# Bookkeeping Revision for Junior Certificate Business Studies

# SHORTCUTS TO SUCCESS

# BOOKKEEPING REVISION FOR JUNIOR CERTIFICATE BUSINESS STUDIES

## SECOND EDITION

Díarmuid Canning and Wynn Oliver

Gill & Macmillan

Gill & Macmillan Ltd
Hume Avenue
Park West
Dublin 12
with associated companies throughout the world
www.gillmacmillan.ie


ISBN-13: 978 0 7171 4115 9
ISBN-10: 0 7171 4115 2
Print origination in Ireland by Carole Lynch

*The paper used in this book is made from the wood pulp of managed forests.
For every tree felled, at least one tree is planted, thereby renewing natural resources.*

This book is dedicated to our parents
Sean and Margaret, Alexander and Gladys
and
Ross, Hollie and Emma
and
All our students over the years

# Contents

## Preface

The aim of this book is to provide a comprehensive approach to bookkeeping in the Junior Certificate examination. Each topic is built up from its most basic components to allow students to revise the appropriate syllabus content regardless of previous knowledge.

It contains fully worked examples built up from the basics as well as fully worked solutions to past examination questions.

Each section has practice questions to allow students to gauge their understanding before moving on to the next section and finally to approach Junior Certificate-style questions. Solutions to these practice questions are available on the internet at www.gillmacmillan.ie.

We hope this reference will help students when both revising and learning bookkeeping for the first time, particularly at higher level Junior Certificate.

Díarmuid Canning MA HDE and Wynn Oliver BSc HDE
Business Faculty
St Andrew's College
Booterstown Avenue
Blackrock
Co. Dublin

## Currency Symbols in this Book

Please note that all currency references before the year 2002 are to Irish Pounds and abbreviated as 'IR£'. Currency references from the year 2002 onwards are to the 'Euro' and abbreviated as '€'.

### Website

Check out the website for this book www.gillmacmillan.ie for solutions to practice questions.

# CHAPTER 1
# FINAL ACCOUNTS OF A PRIVATE LIMITED COMPANY

## Introduction

Every firm needs to know on a regular basis (normally once a year) whether they are making a profit or a loss. **Making a profit is the main aim of business**, therefore it is essential that firms know their financial position and the Final Accounts enable them to do just that.

A firm's final accounts are made up of four sections:

1. Trading Account.
2. Profit and Loss Account.
3. Appropriation Account.
4. Balance Sheet.

But first some important terms.

## Important Terms

### *Trading Period*

The normal trading period for a firm is one year, it can be any twelve month slot (starting on the first day of the first month and ending on the last day of the twelfth month) i.e.

1st February 2003 ⟶ 31st January 2004

### *Revenues and Expenses*

In order to calculate profit it is necessary for a business to find out its total revenues and expenses for the trading period.

**Profit = Revenue – Expenses**

REVENUES

➘ *The money earned by the business through business activities.*

EXPENSES

➘ *The costs of the running the business (excluding the cost of buying goods for resale).*

Both revenues and expenses are divided into two categories.

### *Revenues*

*TRADING REVENUE (TR) — TRADING ACCOUNT*

Any revenue which results directly from the trading activity of the business (i.e. selling goods). An example is:

*Net Sales:* Money earned by selling goods (i.e. sales less sales returns).

*BUSINESS REVENUE (BR) — PROFIT AND LOSS ACCOUNT*

Any other revenue earned by the business. Examples are:

*Rent Received*: Income earned by the business renting premises it owns.
*Commission Received:* Income earned by the business through selling the goods of another company.
*Interest Received:* Interest earned on the business's savings.

### *Expenses*

*TRADING EXPENSES (TE) — TRADING ACCOUNT*

*Net Purchases:* Cost of buying goods (purchases less purchase returns).
*Carriage In:* Cost of transporting purchased goods into the business.
*Customs/Import Duties:* Tax payable on goods imported into the country.
*Manufacturing Wages:* Wages paid to workers manufacturing the goods being purchased.

*BUSINESS EXPENSES (BE) — PROFIT AND LOSS ACCOUNT*

*Wages/Salaries:* Total cost of the workers employed.
*Light and heat:* Total cost of electricity and fuel for heat.
*Rent:* Cost of the premises if not owned by the business.
*Insurance:* Cost of covering the business against various risks.
*Carriage Out:* Cost of delivering goods to customers.

## 1.1 TRADING ACCOUNT

The trading account shows the profit made from buying and selling goods only, it ignores the costs of running the business itself. It is used to calculate the Gross Profit or Gross Loss of a business over a trading period. Simply put, it is trading revenues less trading expenses with allowance made for opening and closing stock.

### Structure

1. *Calculate the value of net sales (Turnover).*
   This includes the amount of money received from selling goods LESS the value of any goods returned to the business (due to faults etc.). These returns are known as Sales Returns or Returns Inwards.

2. *Cost of sales.*

   This is what it cost the business to buy the goods it sold in (1) above.
   It includes the value of goods held in stock/opening stock, (i.e. goods bought in the last time period but not sold in that period) ADD ⬇

   Net Purchases. The monetary value of purchasing goods for resale LESS the value of any goods returned by the business (due to faults etc.) or Purchase Returns (or Returns Outwards) during the time period. ADD ⬇

   Anything that may increase the price paid for these goods. Includes items such as Carriage Inwards, Custom/Import Duties and Manufacturing Wages EQUALS ⬇

   Cost of Goods Available for Sale or what it cost the business to buy the goods it sold in (1) above. LESS ⬇

   Closing Stock, this is the monetary value of goods not sold in this time period. EQUALS COST OF SALES

3. *Gross Profit.*

   Subtract Cost of Sales from Net Sales to get Gross Profit/Loss (i.e. 1–2 = **Gross Profit/Loss**).

*GROSS PROFIT IS PROFIT MADE FROM BUYING AND SELLING GOODS, IT IGNORES THE COSTS OF RUNNING THE BUSINESS.*

### *Example A*

Prepare a Trading Account for McGeady Ltd from the following information as at the 31st December 2001:

| | |
|---|---|
| *Sales* | *IR£292,000* |
| *Sales Returns* | *IR£25,000* |
| *Opening stock* | *IR£13,000* |
| *Purchases* | *IR£200,000* |
| *Purchase Returns* | *IR£10,000* |
| *Carriage Inwards* | *IR£800* |
| *Customs Duties* | *IR£200* |
| *Closing stock* | *IR£15,000* |

| Trading Account for McGeady Ltd year ending 31st December 2001 | | | | |
|---|---|---|---|---|
| | | IR£ | IR£ | IR£ |
| | Sales | | 292,000 | |
| Less | Sales Returns | | 25,000 | 267,000 |
| **Less** | **Cost of Sales** | | | |
| | Opening Stock | | 13,000 | |
| | Purchases | 200,000 | | |
| Less | Purchase Returns | 10,000 | 190,000 | |
| | Carriage In | | 800 | |
| | Customs Duties | | 200 | |
| | Cost of Goods Available for Sale | | 204,000 | |
| Less | Closing Stock | | 15,000 | 189,000 |
| | **GROSS PROFIT** | | | **78,000** |

## Practice Questions

1. Using the information below prepare a ***Trading Account*** for McCann Ltd for the year ended 31st December 2003.

| | |
|---|---|
| *Sales* | *€59,000* |
| *Sales Returns* | *€1,200* |
| *Opening Stock* | *€2,500* |
| *Purchases* | *€37,200* |
| *Purchase Returns* | *€200* |
| *Import Duty* | *€1,800* |
| *Closing Stock* | *€1,800* |

2. Using the information below prepare a ***Trading Account*** for Jones Ltd for the year ended 31st December 2001.

| | |
|---|---|
| *Purchase Returns* | *IR£2,220* |
| *Sales* | *IR£122,000* |
| *Closing Stock* | *IR£990* |
| *Opening Stock* | *IR£50,000* |
| *Carriage In* | *IR£1,750* |
| *Purchases* | *IR£41,500* |

3. Using the information below prepare a ***Trading Account*** for Lewis Ltd for the year ended 31st March 2002.

| | |
|---|---|
| *Opening Stock* | *€1,800* |
| *Carriage In* | *€1,820* |
| *Purchase Returns* | *€1,550* |

| | |
|---|---|
| *Sales Returns* | *€550* |
| *Customs Duty* | *€2,050* |
| *Sales* | *€81,000* |
| *Purchases* | *€55,000* |
| *Closing Stock* | *€710* |

4. Using the information below prepare a ***Trading Account*** for Beere Ltd for the year ended 31st January 2002.

| | |
|---|---|
| *Manufacturing Wages* | *€12,100* |
| *Closing Stock* | *€980* |
| *Purchases* | *€27,000* |
| *Sales Returns* | *€985* |
| *Sales* | *€34,050* |
| *Opening Stock* | *€9,800* |

5. Using the information below prepare a ***Trading Account*** for Duff Ltd for the year ended 31st August 2004.

| | |
|---|---|
| *Closing Stock* | *€19,800* |
| *Import Duty* | *€4,850* |
| *Sales* | *€331,000* |
| *Purchases* | *€73,000* |
| *Sales Returns* | *€5,900* |
| *Purchase Returns* | *€9,050* |
| *Opening Stock* | *€21,050* |
| *Carriage In* | *€5,700* |

## 1.2 PROFIT AI

This account shows … has added other
revenues (business r… ness expenses) —
arriving at a figure f… business revenues
less business expens…

### Structure

1. *Gross Profit*
   As calculated …

2. *Business Reven…*
   This is the tot… by selling goods.
   Includes item… and commission
   received. Bus… the appendage
   'received' or '…

Profit and Loss Account

Structure:
1) Gross Profit
2) Business Revenues/Gains
3) Business Expenses
4) Net Profit

3. *Business Expenses*
   This is the total cost of running the business other than the cost of buying goods for resale. Includes items such as telephone, ESB, wages, stationery etc. EQUALS ⬇

4. *Net Profit*
   This is the profit remaining when all other business revenues and business expenses have been added and deducted from gross profit.

***Example B***

Prepare a Profit and Loss Account for McGeady Ltd from the following information as at the 31st December 2001:

| | |
|---|---|
| *Gross Profit* | *IR£78,000 (taken from Example A)* |
| *Rent received* | *IR£20,000* |
| *Interest received* | *IR£500* |
| *Carriage out* | *IR£1,250* |
| *Stationery* | *IR£2,750* |
| *Light and Heat* | *IR£3,000* |
| *Wages* | *IR£43,000* |
| *Insurance* | *IR£24,750* |

**Profit and Loss Account for McGeady Ltd year ending 31st December 2001**

| | | IR£ | IR£ | IR£ |
|---|---|---|---|---|
| | Gross Profit | | | 78,000 |
| **ADD** | **BUSINESS REVENUES** | | | |
| | Rent received | | 20,000 | |
| | Interest received | | 500 | 20,500 |
| | | | | 98,500 |
| **LESS** | **BUSINESS EXPENSES** | | | |
| | Carriage out | | 1,250 | |
| | Light and Heat | | 3,000 | |
| | Wages | | 43,000 | |
| | Insurance | | 24,750 | 72,000 |
| | **NET PROFIT** | | | **26,500** |

*Figure 1.1 — Summary of Profit and Loss Account for McGeady Ltd year ending 31st December 2001*

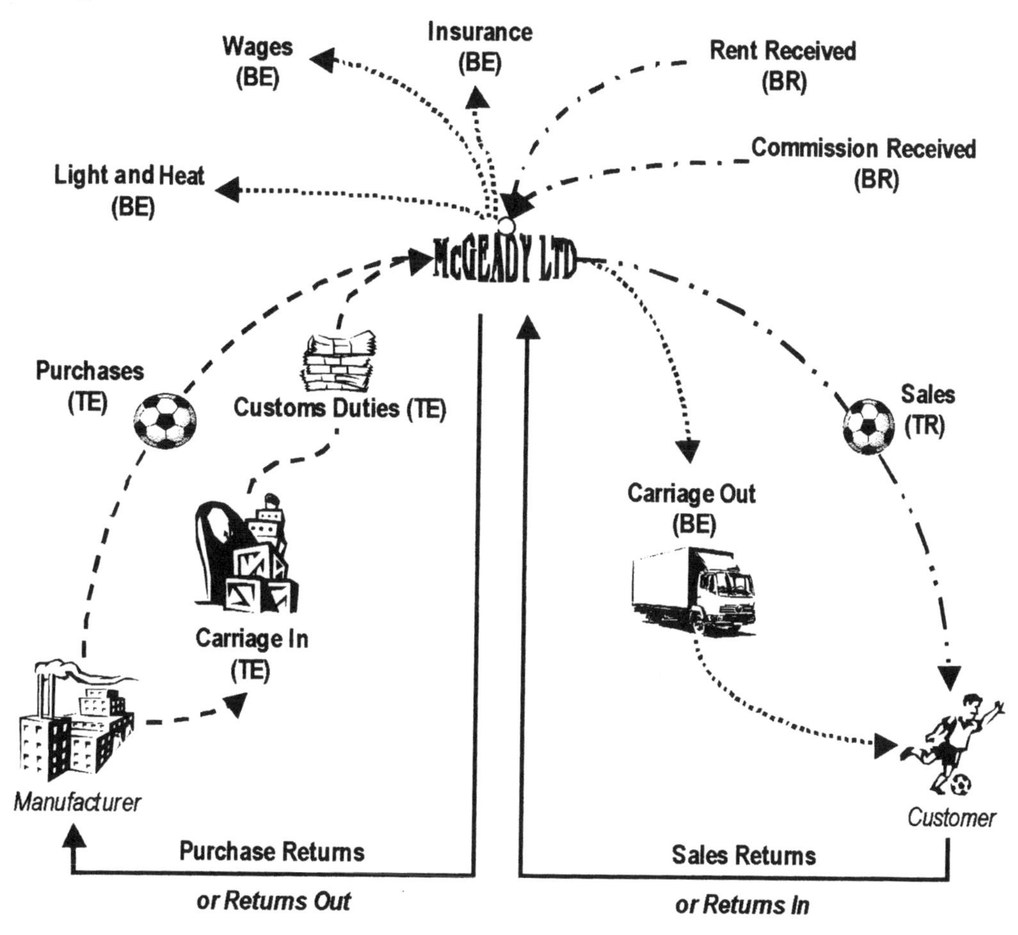


## Practice Questions

1. Using the information below prepare a ***Profit and Loss Account*** for Woods Ltd for the year ended 31st December 2003.

| | |
|---|---|
| *Gross Profit* | *€133,000* |
| *Interest Received* | *€31,200* |
| *Commission Received* | *€2,800* |
| *Wages* | *€43,000* |
| *Light and Heat* | *€8,770* |
| *Carriage Out* | *€4,800* |
| *Insurance* | *€12,000* |
| *Advertising* | *€21,050* |

2. Using the information below prepare a ***Profit and Loss Account*** for Childs Ltd for the year ended 31st December 2004.

| | |
|---|---|
| *ESB* | *€3,500* |
| *Stationery* | *€200* |
| *Loan Interest* | *€350* |
| *Gross Profit* | *€63,000* |
| *Interest Received* | *€1,050* |
| *Carriage Out* | *€380* |

3. Using the information below prepare a ***Profit and Loss Account*** for Hamill Ltd for the year ended 30th April 2005.

| | |
|---|---|
| *Wages* | *€18,000* |
| *Light and Heat* | *€5,500* |
| *Gross Profit* | *€34,000* |
| *Insurance* | *€12,550* |
| *Advertising* | *€8,700* |

4. Using the information below prepare a ***Profit and Loss Account*** for Walshe Ltd for the year ended 31st December 2003.

| | |
|---|---|
| *Wages* | *€12,500* |
| *Loan Interest* | *€570* |
| *Interest Received* | *€950* |
| *Gross Profit* | *€68,900* |
| *Stationery* | *€480* |
| *Carriage Out* | *€2,200* |

5. Using the information below prepare a ***Profit and Loss Account*** for Archer Ltd for the year ended 30th September 2002.

| | |
|---|---|
| *Rent Received* | *€22,000* |
| *Interest Received* | *€5,900* |
| *Gross Profit* | *€133,200* |
| *Insurance* | *€9,000* |
| *Advertising* | *€18,800* |
| *Wages* | *€24,300* |

**BRINGING THE TRADING AND PROFIT AND LOSS ACCOUNTS TOGETHER**

6. Using the information below prepare a ***Trading and Profit and Loss Account*** for Jenkins Ltd for the year ended 31st December 2003.

| | |
|---|---|
| *Sales Returns* | *€5,900* |
| *Wages* | *€22,000* |
| *ESB* | *€1,350* |
| *Purchases* | *€54,000* |

| | |
|---|---|
| *Sales* | *€120,300* |
| *Purchases Returns* | *€700* |
| *Closing Stock* | *€8,050* |
| *Opening Stock* | *€10,500* |
| *Rent Received* | *€7,500* |
| *Carriage In* | *€1,050* |
| *Insurance* | *€2,040* |
| *Loan Interest* | *€870* |

7. Using the information below prepare a ***Trading and Profit and Loss Account*** for Dzifa Ltd for the year ended 31st May 2004.

| | |
|---|---|
| *Sales* | *€80,400* |
| *Advertising* | *€4,050* |
| *Purchases* | *€40,400* |
| *Wages* | *€9,850* |
| *Opening Stock* | *€2,200* |
| *Purchases Returns* | *€700* |
| *Customs Duty* | *€200* |
| *Closing Stock* | *€1,500* |
| *Stationery* | *€345* |

8. Using the information below prepare a ***Trading and Profit and Loss Account*** for Liefe Ltd for the year ended 31st January 2005.

| | |
|---|---|
| *Sales* | *€200,900* |
| *Closing Stock* | *€4,550* |
| *Opening Stock* | *€5,500* |
| *Light and Heat* | *€1,500* |
| *Interest Received* | *€800* |
| *Purchases* | *€120,700* |
| *Carriage In* | *€990* |
| *Sales Returns* | *€3,500* |
| *Rent Received* | *€2,505* |
| *Purchases Returns* | *€5,400* |
| *Wages* | *€15,000* |
| *Insurance* | *€10,100* |

## 1.3 APPROPRIATION ACCOUNT

This account shows how net profit is shared out. The board of directors recommend to shareholders how this should be done. There are three ways a firm can distribute net profit:

1. All net profit is given in the form of an ordinary share dividend to shareholders.
2. All net profit is retained by the firm for use in the future.
3. The net profit is divided between shareholders and firm.

Option 3 is normally used in Junior Certificate questions. Shareholders receive a dividend to show a return on their investment, with the firm keeping the remainder to invest back into the business.

### Structure

1. *Net Profit*

   As calculated in the firm's Profit and Loss account LESS ↓

2. *Dividend*

   The dividend can be presented in one of two ways:

   (a) Dividend Paid — You will be given this figure and it is simply deducted from net profit in the Appropriation Account.

   (b) Dividend Declared/Proposed — You are told the board has decided that a portion of net profit will be paid as a dividend. This is a percentage of **Issued Share Capital**. This figure is then deducted from net profit in the Appropriation Account and *is also a current liability in the Balance Sheet.*

   Either of these figures deducted from net profit EQUALS ↓

3. *Reserves / Retained Earnings*

   This is the amount of net profit kept or retained by the firm for future use.

***Example C (a)***

Prepare Appropriation Account for McGeady Ltd from the following information as at the 31st December 2001:

*Net Profit IR£26,500 (taken from Example B)*
*Dividend Paid IR£12,000*

| Appropriation Account for McGeady Ltd year ending 31st December 2001 | | | |
|---|---|---|---|
| | IR£ | IR£ | IR£ |
| Net Profit | | | 26,500 |
| Less Dividend paid | | | 12,000 |
| Reserves | | | 14,500 |

Reserves will also be included in the Balance Sheet

***Example C (b)***

Prepare Appropriation Account for McGeady Ltd from the following information as at the 31st December 2001:

*Net Profit IR£26,500 (taken from Example B)*
*Dividend declared 12%*
*Issued Share Capital IR£100,000*

**Dividend Calculation**

12% of Issued Share Capital or $\frac{12}{100}$ x £100,000 = £12,000

| Appropriation Account for McGeady Ltd year ending 31st December 2001 | | | |
|---|---|---|---|
| | IR£ | IR£ | IR£ |
| Net Profit | | | 26,500 |
| Less Dividend declared | | | 12,000 |
| Reserves | | | 14,500 |

Both the dividend declared and reserves will also be included in the Balance Sheet.

## Practice Questions

1. Using the information below prepare an ***Appropriation Account*** for Burns Ltd for the year ended 31st October 2006.

| | |
|---|---|
| *Net Profit* | *€34,300* |
| *Dividend Declared* | *12%* |
| *Issued Share Capital* | *€120,000* |

2. Using the information below prepare an ***Appropriation Account*** for Bear Ltd for the year ended 30th June 2004.

| | |
|---|---|
| *Dividend Declared* | *14%* |
| *Net Profit* | *€64,200* |
| *Issued Share Capital* | *€140,000* |

3. Using the information below prepare an ***Appropriation Account*** for Cromwell Ltd for the year ended 31st March 2005.

| | |
|---|---|
| *Net Profit* | *€70,400* |
| *Dividend Declared* | *17%* |
| *Issued Share Capital* | *€200,000* |

4. Using the information below prepare an ***Appropriation Account*** for Smith Ltd for the year ended 31st July 2001.

| | |
|---|---|
| *Net Profit* | *IR£120,600* |
| *Dividend Paid* | *IR£78,200* |

5. Using the information below prepare an ***Appropriation Account*** for Dexter Ltd for the year ended 31st October 2007.

| | |
|---|---|
| *Dividend Declared* | *8%* |
| *Net Profit* | *€41,250* |
| *Issued Share Capital* | *€90,000* |

## BRINGING THE TRADING, PROFIT AND LOSS AND APPROPRIATION ACCOUNTS TOGETHER

6. Using the information below prepare a ***Trading, Profit and Loss and Appropriation Account*** for Johnson Ltd for the year ended 31st March 2005.

| | |
|---|---|
| *Purchases* | *€33,000* |
| *Commission Received* | *€1,950* |
| *Purchase Returns* | *€750* |
| *Customs Duty* | *€17,030* |
| *Opening Stock* | *€17,300* |
| *Sales Returns* | *€500* |
| *Carriage Out* | *€600* |
| *Advertising* | *€1,100* |
| *Sales* | *€87,000* |
| *ESB* | *€21,050* |
| *Closing Stock* | *€9,000* |
| *Issued Share Capital* | *€70,000* |
| *Dividend Declared* | *6%* |

7. Using the information below prepare a ***Trading, Profit and Loss and Appropriation Account*** for Cook Ltd for the year ended 31st August 2006.

| | |
|---|---|
| *Wages* | *€12,000* |
| *Purchases* | *€43,500* |
| *Insurance* | *€10,500* |
| *Purchase Returns* | *€2,500* |
| *Interest Received* | *€950* |
| *Light and Heat* | *€700* |
| *Opening Stock* | *€17,000* |
| *Sales* | *€119,000* |
| *Import Duty* | *€800* |
| *Sales Returns* | *€1,200* |
| *Closing Stock* | *€11,500* |
| *Rent Received* | *€8,500* |
| *Dividend Paid* | *€25,000* |

8. Using the information below prepare a ***Trading, Profit and Loss and Appropriation Account*** for Jennie Ltd for the year ended 30th September 2006.

| | |
|---|---|
| *Insurance* | *€5,500* |
| *Sales* | *€200,300* |
| *Purchases* | *€89,000* |
| *Carriage In* | *€7,700* |
| *Issued Share Capital* | *€300,000* |
| *Closing Stock* | *€15,000* |
| *Wages* | *€34,800* |
| *Sales Returns* | *€2,400* |
| *Stationery* | *€900* |
| *Opening Stock* | *€24,000* |
| *Carriage Out* | *€1,300* |
| *Dividend Declared* | *12%* |

## 1.4 BALANCE SHEET

The Balance Sheet shows everything owned by a firm and everything owed by a firm. In other words, it shows a firm's assets and liabilities. These two categories can be further subdivided.

### Assets (Items owned by a business)

***Fixed Assets*** *(remain constant over a reasonable period of time)*

- Land
- Premises
- Machinery
- Vehicles
- Fixtures and fittings

*Current Assets (regularly change in value and are easily converted into cash)*

- Cash
- Bank
- Debtors — owe firm money
- Stock

## Liabilities (items owed by a business)

*Current Liabilities (owed by the firm in the short-run)*

- Creditors —money owed to them by firm
- Bank overdraft
- Creditors
- Dividend due

*Long-term Liabilities (owed by the firm in the long-run)*

- Long-term loan
- Reserves

*Issued Share Capital*

Junior Certificate questions usually contain both Authorised and Issued Share Capital.

**Authorised Share Capital** — *Total amount of money a firm can raise through selling shares.*

**Issued Share Capital** — *Actual amount of money a firm has raised so far by selling shares.*

**THE FULL BALANCE SHEET IS MADE UP AS FOLLOWS:**

Assets = Liabilities

Fixed Assets + Current Assets = Current Liabilities + Long-term Liabilities + Issued Share Capital

Fixed Assets + (Current Assets – Current Liabilities) = Long-term Liabilities + Issued Share Capital

(Current Assets – Current Liabilities) = Working Capital

Fixed Assets + Working Capital = Total Net Assets

Long-term Liabilities + Issued Share Capital = Capital Employed

**THE BALANCE SHEET SHOWS THAT:**

Total Net Assets = Capital Employed

## Working Capital

The difference between current assets and current liabilities is called WORKING CAPITAL. This is a very important figure taken from the Balance Sheet. A positive working capital means the company has enough current assets to pay off its current liabilities. A negative working capital is a danger signal for a company, it shows the company is short of funds to pay off its most pressing debts. The company is said to be ***overtrading***.

### *Structure*

There are two figures we need: Total Net Assets and Capital Employed.

#### TOTAL NET ASSETS

1. *Fixed Assets*
   Calculate the total value of the firm's fixed assets.
2. *Current Assets*
   LESS ⬇
3. *Current Liabilities*
   EQUALS ⬇
4. *Working Capital*
   Current assets less current liabilities. Working capital is added to total fixed assets to EQUAL ⬇
5. *Total Net Assets*

#### CAPITAL EMPLOYED

6. *Issued Share Capital*
   The value of shares sold PLUS ⬇
7. *Reserves*
   Retained earnings, that part of net profit not paid to shareholders PLUS ⬇
8. *Long-term Liabilities*
   Such as a five year loan EQUALS ⬇
9. *Capital Employed*

***Remember Total Net Assets = Capital Employed***

### *Example D*

Prepare the Balance Sheet for McGeady Ltd from the following information as at the 31st December 2001:

| | |
|---|---|
| *Premises* | *IR£100,000* |
| *Vehicles* | *IR£28,000* |
| *Cash in hand* | *IR£12,000* |
| *Closing stock* | *IR£15,000* |
| *Bank overdraft* | *IR£6,500* |
| *Dividend declared* | *IR£12,000 (taken from Example C)* |
| *Long-term loan* | *IR£22,000* |
| *Reserves* | *IR£14,500 (taken from Example C)* |
| *Issued Share Capital* | *IR£100,000* |

*McGeady Ltd has an Authorised Share Capital of 200,000 IR£1 ordinary shares.*

| Balance Sheet for McGeady Ltd as at 31st December 2001 | | | |
|---|---|---|---|
| | IR£ | IR£ | IR£ |
| **Fixed Assets** | | | |
| Premises | | 100,000 | |
| Vehicles | | 28,000 | 128,000 |
| **Current Assets** | | | |
| Cash in Hand | 12,000 | | |
| Closing Stock | 15,000 | 27,000 | |
| **Less** **Current Liabilities** | | | |
| Bank Overdraft | 6,500 | | |
| Dividend declared | 12,000 | 18,500 | |
| Working Capital | | | 8,500 |
| **TOTAL NET ASSETS** | | | **136,500** |
| **FINANCED BY** | | | |
| Authorised and Issued Share Capital | | 200,000 | 100,000 |
| **Add** **Long-term Liabilities** | | | |
| Long-term loan | | 22,000 | |
| Reserves | | 14,500 | 36,500 |
| **CAPITAL EMPLOYED** | | | **136,500** |

**Notes**

- *The title of the account 'as at 31st December 2001...' is different to 'year ending 31st December 2001...' as in the Trading, Profit and Loss and Appropriation Accounts. This is because the Balance Sheet shows a view of the business at one point in time. The Trading, Profit and Loss and Appropriation Accounts show what has been going on throughout the trading period. It may be useful to think of the Trading, Profit and Loss and Appropriation as a videotape and the Balance Sheet as a photograph.*
- *We include the Authorised Share Capital amount in the 'Financed By' section of the Balance Sheet but the figure is not used in our calculations. It is there for information and legal purposes only.*

## Practice Questions

1. Using the information below prepare a ***Balance Sheet*** for KIMJ Ltd for the year ended 30th September 2006. KIMJ Ltd has an Authorised Share Capital of 400,000 €1 ordinary shares.

| | |
|---|---|
| *Closing Stock* | *€2,300* |
| *Issued Share Capital* | *€190,000* |
| *Creditors* | *€4,800* |
| *Bank* | *€19,000* |

| | |
|---|---|
| *Premises* | *€200,000* |
| *Debtors* | *€8,700* |
| *Dividend Due* | *€10,200* |
| *Long-term Loan* | *€25,000* |

2. Using the information below prepare a ***Balance Sheet*** for Nicki Ltd for the year ended 31st March 2007. Nicki Ltd has an Authorised Share Capital of 400,000 €1 ordinary shares.

| | |
|---|---|
| *Bank Overdraft* | *€900* |
| *Land* | *€120,000* |
| *Issued Share Capital* | *€150,000* |
| *Closing Stock* | *€21,500* |
| *Debtors* | *€11,000* |
| *Dividend Due* | *€31,000* |
| *Equipment* | *€72,000* |
| *Creditors* | *€1,500* |
| *Reserves* | *€41,100* |

3. Using the information below prepare a ***Balance Sheet*** for Eric Ltd for the year ended 31st December 2004. Eric Ltd has an Authorised Share Capital of 300,000 €1 ordinary shares.

| | |
|---|---|
| *Premises* | *€115,000* |
| *Closing Stock* | *€27,000* |
| *Dividend Due* | *€15,000* |
| *Issued Share Capital* | *€100,000* |
| *Cash* | *€3,000* |
| *Long-term Loan* | *€50,000* |
| *Debtors* | *€43,000* |
| *Creditors* | *€54,500* |
| *Machinery* | *€55,000* |
| *Reserves* | *€23,500* |

4. Using the information below prepare a ***Balance Sheet*** for Roy Ltd for the year ended 31st January 2005. Roy Ltd has an Authorised Share Capital of 500,000 €1 ordinary shares.

| | |
|---|---|
| *Fixtures and Fittings* | *€9,000* |
| *Premises* | *€124,000* |
| *Reserves* | *€45,300* |
| *Closing Stock* | *€21,000* |
| *Debtors* | *€14,000* |
| *Equipment* | *€57,000* |
| *Creditors* | *€13,800* |

| | |
|---|---|
| *Issued Share Capital* | *€120,000* |
| *Bank Overdraft* | *€11,200* |
| *Long-term Loan* | *€34,700* |

5. Using the information below prepare a ***Balance Sheet*** for Calvin Ltd for the year ended 31st December 2006. Calvin Ltd has an Authorised Share Capital of 1,000,000 €1 ordinary shares.

| | |
|---|---|
| *Premises* | *€230,000* |
| *Reserves* | *€61,500* |
| *Dividend Due* | *€40,050* |
| *Closing Stock* | *€59,000* |
| *Creditors* | *€61,800* |
| *Debtors* | *€61,350* |
| *Cash* | *€13,150* |
| *Machinery* | *€120,000* |
| *Bank Overdraft* | *€21,150* |
| *Issued Share Capital* | *€250,000* |
| *Long-term Loan* | *€49,000* |

***Now let's put Examples A, B, C(b) and D together as one question.***

McGeady Ltd is a sports company. Its Authorised Share Capital is 200,000 IR£1 ordinary shares.

The following Trial Balance has been taken from the books of McGeady Ltd as at 31st December 2001, the end of the financial year.

**Trial Balance for McGeady Ltd as at 31st December 2001**

| | IR£ DR | IR£ CR |
|---|---|---|
| Sales | | 292,000 |
| Sales Returns | 25,000 | |
| Opening Stock | 13,000 | |
| Purchases | 200,000 | |
| Purchase Returns | | 10,000 |
| Carriage Inwards | 800 | |
| Customs Duties | 200 | |
| Rent Received | | 20,000 |
| Interest Received | | 500 |
| Carriage Out | 1,250 | |
| Wages | 43,000 | |
| Light and Heat | 3,000 | |
| Insurance | 24,750 | |

| Trial Balance for McGeady Ltd as at 31st December 2001 *contd.* | | |
|---|---|---|
| | IR£<br>DR | IR£<br>CR |
| Premises | 100,000 | |
| Vehicles | 28,000 | |
| Cash in hand | 12,000 | |
| Bank overdraft | | 6,500 |
| Long-term Loan | | 22,000 |
| Issued Share Capital | | 100,000 |
| | 451,000 | 451,000 |

Closing Stock at 31st December 2001 was IR£15,000.
Board of Directors declared a 12% dividend.

From the above figures, prepare a:

(i) Trading Account
(ii) Profit and Loss Account
(iii) Appropriation Account for the year ended 31st December 2001
(iv) Balance Sheet as on that date

| Trading, Profit and Loss and Appropriation Accounts for McGeady Ltd year ending 31st December 2001 | | | | |
|---|---|---|---|---|
| | | IR£ | IR£ | IR£ |
| | Sales | | 292,000 | |
| Less | Sales Returns | | 25,000 | 267,000 |
| **LESS** | **COST OF SALES** | | | |
| | Opening Stock | | 13,000 | |
| | Purchases | 200,000 | | |
| Less | Purchase Returns | 10,000 | 190,000 | |
| | Carriage In | | 800 | |
| | Customs Duties | | 200 | |
| | Cost of Goods Available for Sale | | 204,000 | |
| Less | Closing Stock | | 15,000 | 189,000 |
| | **GROSS PROFIT** | | | 78,000 |
| **ADD** | **BUSINESS REVENUES** | | | |
| | Rent received | | 20,000 | |
| | Interest received | | 500 | 20,500 |
| | | | | 98,500 |

| **Trading, Profit and Loss and Appropriation Accounts for McGeady Ltd year ending 31st December 2001 *contd.*** | | | | |
|---|---|---|---|---|
| | | **IR£** | **IR£** | **IR£** |
| **LESS** | **BUSINESS EXPENSES** | | | |
| | Carriage out | | 1,250 | |
| | Light and Heat | | 3,000 | |
| | Wages | | 43,000 | |
| | Insurance | | 24,750 | 72,000 |
| | **NET PROFIT** | | | **26,500** |
| Less | Dividend declared (12%) | | | 12,000 |
| | **RESERVES** | | | **14,500** |

| **Balance Sheet for McGeady Ltd as at 31st December 2001** | | | | |
|---|---|---|---|---|
| | | **IR£** | **IR£** | **IR£** |
| **FIXED ASSETS** | | | | |
| | Premises | | 100,000 | |
| | Vehicles | | 28,000 | 128,000 |
| **CURRENT ASSETS** | | | | |
| | Cash in Hand | 12,000 | | |
| | Closing Stock | 15,000 | 27,000 | |
| **LESS** | **CURRENT LIABILITIES** | | | |
| | Bank Overdraft | 6,500 | | |
| | Dividend declared | 12,000 | 18,500 | |
| | Working Capital | | | 8,500 |
| | **TOTAL NET ASSETS** | | | **136,500** |
| **FINANCED BY** | | | | |
| | Authorised and Issued Share Capital | | 200,000 | 100,000 |
| **ADD** | **LONG-TERM LIABILITIES** | | | |
| | Long-term loan | | 22,000 | |
| | Reserves | | 14,500 | 36,500 |
| | **CAPITAL EMPLOYED** | | | **136,500** |

## Trial Balance Explained

The Trial Balance is made up of a debit and a credit column. The debit column contains Assets and Expenses, while the credit column contains Liabilities and Revenues.

| Trial Balance as at 31st December 2000 | | |
|---|---|---|
| | DR<br>IR£<br>*Assets*<br>*Expenses* | CR<br>IR£<br>*Liabilities*<br>*Revenues* |

This rule is particularly useful as sometimes students get confused as to whether an item is an expense or a revenue. The classic example that sometimes arises is interest. This could be interest paid on a deposit account, in which case it would appear in the credit column as it is a revenue. However, it could be interest paid on an overdraft, in which case it would appear in the debit column as it is an expense.

## Practice Questions

1. Godsil Ltd is a management company. Its Authorised Share Capital is 400,000 €1 ordinary shares.
   The following Trial Balance has been taken from the books of Godsil Ltd as at 31st December 2004, the end of the financial year.

| Trial Balance for Godsil Ltd as at 31st December 2004 | | |
|---|---|---|
| | €<br>DR | €<br>CR |
| Cash Sales | | 295,000 |
| Opening Stock | 58,900 | |
| Purchases for resale | 278,000 | |
| Interest on Overdraft | 730 | |
| ESB | 8,750 | |
| Wages | 13,000 | |
| Carriage Out | 800 | |
| Insurance | 4,300 | |
| Equipment | 43,000 | |
| Bank Overdraft | | 4,060 |
| Carriage In | 1,800 | |
| Dividend Paid | 8,000 | |
| Premises | 121,000 | |
| Cash in Hand | 780 | |
| Issued Share Capital | | 240,000 |
| | 539,060 | 539,060 |

Closing Stock at 31st December 2004 was €87,000.

From the above figures prepare the following:

(i) Trading Account
(ii) Profit and Loss Account
(iii) Appropriation Account for the year ended 31st December 2004
(iv) Balance Sheet as on that date

2. Hay Ltd is a publishing company. Its Authorised Share Capital is 200,000 €1 ordinary shares.
The following Trial Balance has been taken from the books of Hay Ltd as at 31st December 2006, the end of the financial year.

| Trial Balance for Hay Ltd as at 31st December 2006 | | |
|---|---|---|
| | € DR | € CR |
| Opening Stock | 21,500 | |
| Purchases for resale | 101,200 | |
| Customs Duty | 950 | |
| Sales | | 175,000 |
| Carriage Out | 900 | |
| Debtors | 38,800 | |
| Creditors | | 17,000 |
| Advertising | 1,850 | |
| Commission Received | | 13,000 |
| Salaries | 20,000 | |
| Light and Heat | 600 | |
| Land | 80,000 | |
| Machinery | 35,000 | |
| Bank | 24,200 | |
| Issued Share Capital | | 120,000 |
| | 325,000 | 325,000 |

Closing Stock at 31st December 2006 was €18,200.
Board of Directors declared a 14% dividend.

From the above figures prepare the following:

(i) Trading Account
(ii) Profit and Loss Account
(iii) Appropriation Account for the year ended 31st December 2006
(iv) Balance Sheet as on that date

3. Burns Ltd is a consultancy company. Its Authorised Share Capital is 150,000 €1 ordinary shares.
The following Trial Balance has been taken from the books of Burns Ltd as at 31st December 2003, the end of the financial year.

| Trial Balance for Burns Ltd as at 31st December 2003 | | |
|---|---|---|
| | € DR | € CR |
| Sales | | 282,000 |
| Opening Stock | 20,000 | |
| Purchases | 210,000 | |
| Carriage In | 950 | |
| Rent Received | | 12,000 |
| Sales Returns | 13,000 | |
| Purchase Returns | | 4,500 |
| Fixtures and Fittings | 13,000 | |
| Cash | 10,000 | |
| Bank Overdraft | | 21,050 |
| Wages and Salaries | 40,000 | |
| Insurance | 8,000 | |
| Light and Heat | 5,550 | |
| Equipment | 75,000 | |
| Debtors | 17,050 | |
| Creditors | | 9,000 |
| Issued Share Capital | | 84,000 |
| | 412,550 | 412,550 |

Closing Stock at 31st December 2003 was €18,000.
Board of Directors declared a 20% dividend.

From the above figures prepare the following:

(i) Trading Account
(ii) Profit and Loss Account
(iii) Appropriation Account for the year ended 31st December 2003
(iv) Balance Sheet as on that date

4. Reeves Ltd is a computer component company. Its Authorised Share Capital is 400,000 €1 ordinary shares.
The following Trial Balance has been taken from the books of Reeves Ltd as at 31st December 2008, the end of the financial year.

| Trial Balance for Reeves Ltd as at 31st December 2008 | | |
|---|---|---|
| | € DR | € CR |
| Sales Returns | 3,700 | |
| Purchases | 178,000 | |
| Import Duty | 900 | |
| Light and Heat | 2,300 | |
| Opening Stock | 39,500 | |
| Advertising | 5,500 | |
| Purchase Returns | | 5,700 |
| Bank | 23,000 | |
| Creditors | | 6,300 |
| Sales | | 274,000 |
| Salaries | 21,000 | |
| Insurance | 7,700 | |
| Premises | 90,000 | |
| Vehicles | 43,000 | |
| Debtors | 21,400 | |
| Issued Share Capital | | 150,000 |
| | 436,000 | 436,000 |

Closing Stock at 31st December 2008 was €42,200.
Board of Directors declared a 14% dividend.

From the above figures prepare the following:

(i) Trading Account
(ii) Profit and Loss Account
(iii) Appropriation Account for the year ended 31st December 2008
(iv) Balance Sheet as on that date

5. Mathews Ltd is a publishing company. Its Authorised Share Capital is 500,000 €1 ordinary shares.
The following Trial Balance has been taken from the books of Matthews Ltd as at 31st December 2003, the end of the financial year.

| Trial Balance for Mathews Ltd as at 31st December 2003 | | |
|---|---|---|
| | € DR | € CR |
| Sales | | 470,000 |
| Purchases | 389,000 | |
| Carriage In | 12,300 | |
| Opening Stock | 34,300 | |
| Interest Paid | 2,300 | |
| Rent Received | | 43,000 |
| Equipment | 45,000 | |
| Purchase Returns | | 10,400 |
| Light and Heat | 8,900 | |
| Manufacturing Wages | 29,000 | |
| Commission Received | | 19,000 |
| Salaries | 49,000 | |
| Insurance | 14,700 | |
| Buildings | 120,000 | |
| Cash | 7,800 | |
| Debtors | 49,700 | |
| Bank Overdraft | | 5,300 |
| Creditors | | 14,300 |
| Issued Share Capital | | 200,000 |
| | 762,000 | 762,000 |

Closing Stock at 31st December 2003 was €41,200.
Board of Directors declared a 12% dividend.

From the above figures prepare the following:

(i) Trading Account
(ii) Profit and Loss Account
(iii) Appropriation Account for the year ended 31st December 2003
(iv) Balance Sheet as on that date

## 1.5 ADJUSTMENTS TO FINAL ACCOUNTS

In order to get a truer picture of a business it is necessary to make certain adjustments to a firm's Final Accounts. The following adjustments may have to be made at Higher Level:

- *Accruals (amounts due to the firm or by the firm)*
- *Prepayments (amounts paid in advance)*
- *Depreciation (straight-line)*

- *Closing stock*
- *Dividend declared*

Adjustments are not included in the Trial Balance but they must be included in the final accounts twice, one entry will be in the Trading, Profit and Loss or Appropriation Accounts and the other entry will be in the Balance Sheet.

## Accruals

### *Accrued Revenues (revenues due to the business)*

This is any income for the trading period that has not yet been received. Even though it has not yet been paid to the firm, it must be entered in the Final Accounts for the trading period in which it fell due. All revenues received plus all revenues due to be received are included in the accounts for this trading period. As the firm expects to receive these revenues shortly they are also included as a current asset in the Balance Sheet. Examples are rent receivable due, interest receivable due etc...

- ***ADD*** *the amount due to the amount already received in the* ***Revenues*** *section of the* ***Profit and Loss Account.***
- *Record the amount due to be received as a* ***Current Asset*** *in the* ***Balance Sheet.***

***Example***

*Rent received IR£26,000*
*Rent receivable due IR£4,000* } *For the year ending 31st January 2001*
*Interest received IR£2,500*

| Profit and Loss Account Extract for year ending 31st January 2001 | | | | |
|---|---|---|---|---|
| | | IR£ | IR£ | IR£ |
| | **BUSINESS REVENUES** | | | |
| | Rent received | 26,000 | | |
| Add | Rent receivable due | 4,000 | 30,000 | |
| | Interest received | | 2,500 | 32,500 |

| Balance Sheet Extract as at 31st January 2001 | | | |
|---|---|---|---|
| | IR£ | IR£ | IR£ |
| **CURRENT ASSETS** | | | |
| Rent receivable due | | 4,000 | |

### *Accrued Expenses (expenses due by the business)*

All expenses due by a business relating to a trading period must be included in the Final Accounts, whether they have been paid or not. Even though these expenses have not been paid during this trading period, they are due for services rendered during this time period and therefore must be added to the expenses already paid. As the firm is yet to pay these expenses they are also included as a current liability in the Balance Sheet. Examples are Insurance due, ESB due etc...

- ► ***ADD** the amount due to the amount already paid in the **Expenses** section of the **Profit and Loss Account.***
- ► *Record the amount due as a **Current Liability** in the **Balance Sheet.***

***Example***

*Insurance IR£4,750*
*ESB IR£9,655*
*ESB due IR£3,500*
} *For the year ending 31st March 2001*

| Profit and Loss Account Extract for year ending 31st March 2001 | | | | |
|---|---|---|---|---|
| | | IR£ | IR£ | IR£ |
| | **BUSINESS EXPENSES** | | | |
| | Insurance | | 4,750 | |
| | ESB | 9,655 | | |
| Add | ESB due | 3,500 | 13,155 | 17,905 |

| Balance Sheet Extract as at 31st March 2001 | | | |
|---|---|---|---|
| | IR£ | IR£ | IR£ |
| **CURRENT LIABILITIES** | | | |
| ESB Due | | 3,500 | |

## Prepayments

### *Made to the Business*

In this situation the business receives payment before it is due. This applies to revenues paid in advance in the Profit and Loss Account. The prepayment is deducted from the revenue already received. As the service being paid for has not been provided in this trading period, a prepayment made to a business is also included as a current liability in the Balance Sheet.

- ► *Deduct prepayment from the **Revenue** received in the **Profit and Loss Account.***
- ► *Show the prepayment as a **Current Liability** in the **Balance Sheet.***

***Example***

*Rent received IR£12,000*
*Rent receivable prepaid IR£2,000*
*Interest received IR£3,000*
} *For the year ending 31st January 2001*

| Profit and Loss Account Extract for year ending 31st January 2001 | | | | |
|---|---|---|---|---|
| | | IR£ | IR£ | IR£ |
| | **BUSINESS REVENUES** | | | |
| | Rent received | 12,000 | | |
| Less | Rent receivable prepaid | 2,000 | 10,000 | |
| | Interest received | | 3,000 | 13,000 |

| Balance Sheet Extract as at 31st January 2001 | | | | |
|---|---|---|---|---|
| | | IR£ | IR£ | IR£ |
| | **CURRENT LIABILITIES** | | | |
| | Rent receivable prepaid | | 2,000 | |

*Made by the Business*

In this situation the business pays money in advance, in other words it pays in this trading period for services to be supplied in the next trading period. We only put expenses relevant to the trading period into the Profit and Loss Account, any prepayments made by the business are deducted. Prepayments made by the business are also included as current assets in the Balance Sheet as the service prepaid for has not been used yet.

- ► *Deduct prepayment from the **expense** paid in the **Profit and Loss Account.***
- ► *Show the prepayment as a **Current Asset** in the **Balance Sheet.***

*Example*

*Insurance IR£15,000*
*Insurance prepaid IR£2,500* } *For the year ending 31st March 2001*
*ESB IR£4,000*

| Profit and Loss Account Extract for year ending 31st March 2001 | | | | |
|---|---|---|---|---|
| | | IR£ | IR£ | IR£ |
| | **BUSINESS EXPENSES** | | | |
| | Insurance | 15,000 | | |
| Less | Insurance prepaid | 2,500 | 12,500 | |
| | ESB | | 4,000 | 16,500 |

| Balance Sheet Extract as at 31st March 2001 | | | | |
|---|---|---|---|---|
| | | IR£ | IR£ | IR£ |
| | **CURRENT ASSETS** | | | |
| | Insurance prepaid | | 2,500 | |

## Depreciation (Straight-Line)

As an asset is used, its value is reduced, we call this depreciation. For example as a car is used its resale value falls (e.g. a 1999 Mazda MX3 sells for more than a 1997 Mazda MX3, the 1997 car has depreciated over time, as it has been used). For our purposes we calculate what is called Straight-line Depreciation. This is simply a percentage of the cost of an asset. The reduction or depreciation is considered an expense in the Profit and Loss Account. The depreciation is also deducted from the cost of the fixed asset in the Balance Sheet to give the asset a revised value at the end of the trading period (Net Book Value).

The Balance Sheet now looks slightly different. The figure columns for Fixed Assets are now headed as follows:

1. Cost: The Cost of a fixed asset as listed in the Trial Balance
2. Depreciation: As calculated as an expense in the Profit and Loss Account
3. Net Book Value: Difference between Cost and Depreciation (1–2)

*Figure 1.2*

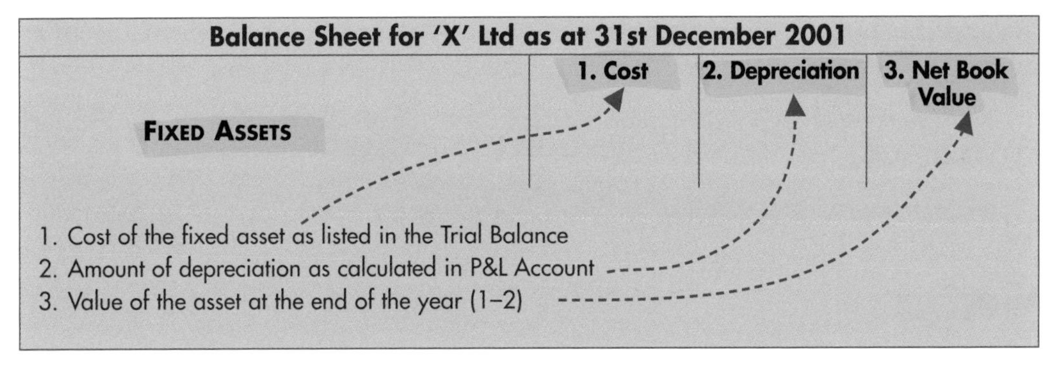


► *Show depreciation (not the full value of the asset) as an **Expense** in the **Profit and Loss Account.***

► *Deduct depreciation from the cost of the asset in the **Fixed Assets** section of the **Balance Sheet.***

***Example***

*Premises IR£45,000*
*Machinery IR£15,000*
*10% depreciation on premises*
*15% depreciation on machinery*

} *For the year ending 31st December 2001*

| Profit and Loss Account Extract for year ending 31st December 2001 | | | |
|---|---|---|---|
| | **IR£** | **IR£** | **IR£** |
| **BUSINESS EXPENSES** | | | |
| Depreciation on premises (10%) | | 4,500 | |
| Depreciation on machinery (15%) | | 2,250 | 6,750 |

| Balance Sheet Extract as at 31st December 2001 | | | |
|---|---|---|---|
| | **Cost** | **Deprec.** | **NBV** |
| **FIXED ASSETS** | | | |
| Premises | 45,000 | 4,500 | 40,500 |
| Machinery | 15,000 | 2,250 | 12,750 |
| | 60,000 | 6,750 | 53,250 |

## Closing Stock

We have already dealt with closing stock. We deduct it from Cost of Goods Available for Sale to get Cost of Sales. It is also included as a current asset in the Balance Sheet as it represents assets that may be turned into cash in the next trading period.

- ► *Closing stock is deducted from Cost of Goods Available for Sale in the Trading Account.*
- ► *Show closing stock as a Current Asset in the Balance Sheet.*

## Dividends

We have already dealt with dividends paid and declared. If a dividend is declared by the Board of a company, it means they have decided the amount of the dividend but it is yet to be paid. The dividend declared is deducted from Net Profit to give Reserves. It is also a Current Liability in the Balance Sheet as it is owed to shareholders (the amount has been decided on but not yet paid).

- ► *Dividend declared is deducted from Net Profit in the Appropriation Account.*
- ► *Show dividend declared as a Current Liability in the Balance Sheet.*

***Example***

*Net Profit IR£45,000*
*Ordinary Share Capital IR£100,000* } *For the year ending 31st March 2001*
*Dividend declared 10%*

| Appropriation Account for year ending 31st March 2001 | | | |
|---|---|---|---|
| | IR£ | IR£ | IR£ |
| Net Profit | | | 45,000 |
| Dividend declared (10%) | | | 10,000 |
| Reserves | | | 35,000 |

| Balance Sheet Extract as at 31st March 2001 | | | |
|---|---|---|---|
| | Cost | Deprec. | NBV |
| **CURRENT LIABILITIES** | | | |
| Dividend declared | | 10,000 | |

## Summary

*Figure 1.3 — Summary of Adjustments to Final Accounts*

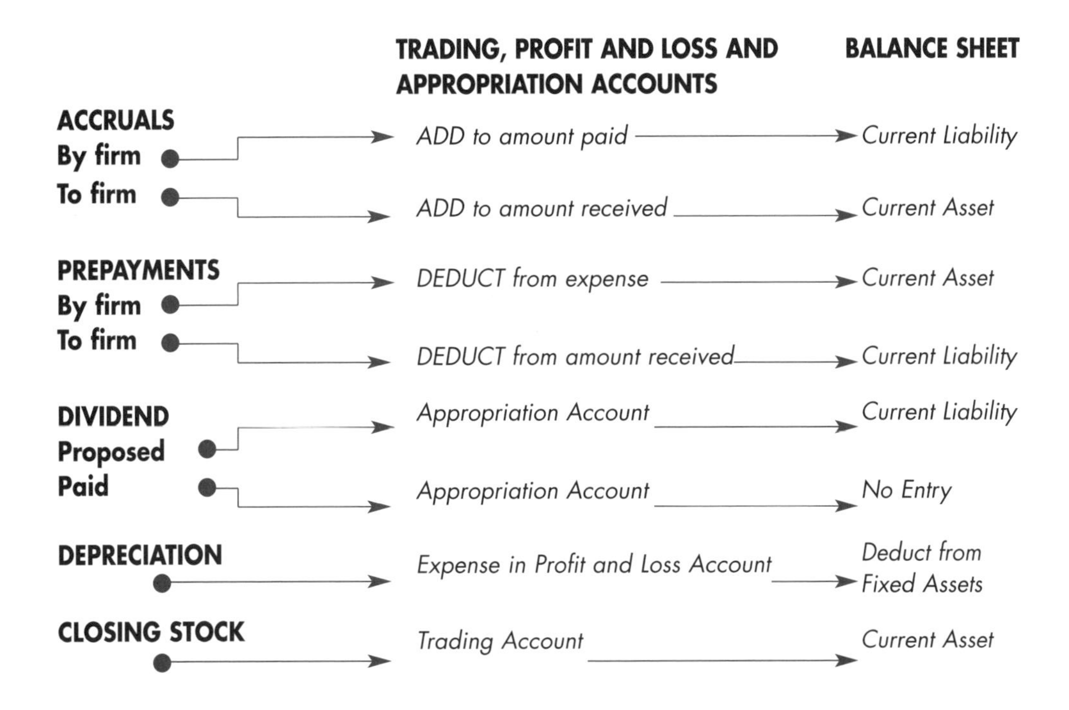


## 1999 Junior Certificate Question and Solution

4. **This is a Final Account and Balance Sheet Question.**
   The following balances were extracted from the books of Brady Ltd on 31st May, 1999. The Authorised Share Capital is 250,000 IR£1 Ordinary Shares.

   You are required to prepare the company's **Profit and Loss and Appropriation Account** for the year ended 31st May, 1999 and a **Balance Sheet** as at that date.

| | IR£ |
|---|---|
| Gross Profit | 96,000 |
| Insurance | 6,400 |
| Rent receivable | 13,400 |
| Debtors | 14,700 |
| Creditors | 16,300 |
| Wages | 13,200 |
| Carriage Outwards | 4,400 |
| Loan Interest | 2,500 |
| Advertising | 7,800 |
| Buildings | 140,000 |
| Machinery | 98,000 |
| Furniture and Fittings | 56,000 |
| Reserves (Profit and Loss Balance) | 40,000 |
| Issued Share Capital 160,000 IR£1 shares | 160,000 |
| Cash | 3,000 |
| Bank Overdraft | 7,300 |
| Long Term Loan | 25,000 |

You are given the following information as at 31st May, 1999:

(i) Closing Stock IR£12,000
(ii) Rent receivable prepaid IR£2,400
(iii) Wages due IR£1,800
(iv) Dividend declared 6%
(v) Depreciation: Machinery 15%, Furniture and Fittings 10% (35)

SOLUTION

**Profit and Loss and Appropriation Account for Brady Ltd year ending 31st May 1999**

| | | IR£ | IR£ | IR£ |
|---|---|---|---|---|
| | **GROSS PROFIT** | | | 96,000 |
| **ADD** | **BUSINESS REVENUES** | | | |
| | Rent Receivable | | 13,400 | |
| Less | Rent Receivable Prepaid | | 2,400 | 11,000 |
| | | | | 107,000 |
| **LESS** | **BUSINESS EXPENSES** | | | |
| | Insurance | | 6,400 | |
| | Wages | 13,200 | | |
| *Add* | Wages Due | 1,800 | 15,000 | |
| | Carriage Outwards | | 4,400 | |
| | Loan Interest | | 2,500 | |
| | Advertising | | 7,800 | |

| Profit and Loss and Appropriation Account for Brady Ltd *contd.* | | | | |
|---|---|---|---|---|
| | | IR£ | IR£ | IR£ |
| | *Depreciation* | | | |
| | Machinery | 14,700 | | |
| | Furniture and Fittings | 5,600 | 20,300 | 56,400 |
| | **NET PROFIT** | | | **50,600** |
| *Add* | Profit and Loss Balance | | | 40,000 |
| | | | | 90,600 |
| Less | Dividend declared (6%) | | | 9,600 |
| | **RESERVES** | | | **81,000** |

| Balance Sheet for Brady Ltd as at 31st May 1999 | | | | |
|---|---|---|---|---|
| | | IR£ | IR£ | IR£ |
| **FIXED ASSETS** | | | | |
| | Buildings | 140,000 | | 140,000 |
| | Machinery | 98,000 | 14,700 | 83,300 |
| | Furniture and Fittings | 56,000 | 5,600 | 50,400 |
| **CURRENT ASSETS** | | 294,000 | 20,300 | 273,700 |
| | Debtors | 14,700 | | |
| | Cash | 3,000 | | |
| | Closing Stock | 12,000 | 29,700 | |
| **LESS** | **CURRENT LIABILITIES** | | | |
| | Creditors | 16,300 | | |
| | Bank Overdraft | 7,300 | | |
| | Rent Receivable Prepaid | 2,400 | | |
| | Wages Due | 1,800 | | |
| | Dividend Declared | 9,600 | 37,400 | (7,700) |
| | **TOTAL NET ASSETS** | | | **266,000** |
| **FINANCED BY** | | Authorised | Issued | |
| | Share Capital | 250,000 | 160,000 | |
| | Reserves | | 81,000 | 241,000 |
| **ADD** | **LONG TERM LIABILITIES** | | | |
| | Long Term Loan | | | 25,000 |
| | **CAPITAL EMPLOYED** | | | **266,000** |

## 1.6 COMBINATION QUESTIONS

1. The following Trial Balance was extracted for the books of Quinn Ltd on the 31st December 2001. The Authorised Share Capital is 200,000 IR£1 ordinary shares.
   You are required to prepare the company's Trading, Profit and Loss and Appropriation Accounts for the year ended 31st December 2001 and a Balance Sheet as at that date.

| | IR£<br>DR | IR£<br>CR |
|---|---|---|
| Sales | | 110,000 |
| Opening Stock | 22,000 | |
| Purchases | 89,500 | |
| Purchase Returns | | 3,000 |
| Sales Returns | 2,000 | |
| Insurance | 5,100 | |
| Machinery | 60,000 | |
| 10 Year Loan | | 30,000 |
| Fixtures and Fittings | 20,000 | |
| Stationery | 300 | |
| Import Duty | 800 | |
| Rent Received | | 10,000 |
| Wages | 10,000 | |
| Light and Heat | 2,000 | |
| Cash on Hand | 3,300 | |
| Debtors | 15,500 | |
| Creditors | | 3,500 |
| Issued Share Capital | | 74,000 |
| | 230,500 | 230,500 |

You are given the following information as at 31st December 2001:

(i) Closing Stock IR£27,300
(ii) Dividends declared 10%
(iii) Rent Received Due IR£2,000
(iv) Wages Due IR£1,300
(v) Insurance Due IR£700
(vi) Depreciation: Machinery 6%

2. The following Trial Balance was extracted for the books of Annie and Sammy Ltd on the 31st December 2008. The Authorised Share Capital is 200,000 €1 ordinary shares.
   You are required to prepare the company's Trading, Profit and Loss and Appropriation Accounts for the year ended 31st December 2008 and a Balance Sheet as at that date.

| | € DR | € CR |
|---|---|---|
| Opening Stock | 49,000 | |
| Purchases | 189,000 | |
| Customs Duty | 7,700 | |
| Rent Received | | 14,000 |
| Commission Received | | 5,500 |
| Sales | | 300,000 |
| Light and Heat | 4,400 | |
| Sales Returns | 7,600 | |
| Premises | 120,000 | |
| Creditors | | 15,300 |
| Purchase Returns | | 9,200 |
| Bank Overdraft | | 7,400 |
| Salaries | 22,000 | |
| Carriage Out | 2,200 | |
| Insurance | 4,200 | |
| Vehicles | 30,000 | |
| Debtors | 10,300 | |
| Issued Share Capital | | 95,000 |
| | 446,400 | 446,400 |

You are given the following information as at 31st December 2008:

(i) Closing Stock €37,800
(ii) Customs Duty Due €1,000
(iii) Rent Received Due €300
(iv) Insurance Prepaid €700
(v) Depreciation: Premises 4%, Vehicles 10%
(vi) Dividend Declared 12%

3. The following Trial Balance was extracted for the books of Rossco Ltd on the 31st December 2007. The Authorised Share Capital is 100,000 €1 ordinary shares.
   You are required to prepare the company's Trading, Profit and Loss and Appropriation Accounts for the year ended 31st December 2007 and a Balance Sheet as at that date.

| | € DR | € CR |
|---|---|---|
| Sales Returns | 2,200 | |
| Carriage In | 5,000 | |
| Commission Received | | 15,000 |
| Sales | | 195,000 |
| Opening Stock | 27,300 | |
| Advertising | 1,800 | |
| Fixtures and Fittings | 17,000 | |
| Debtors | 14,030 | |
| Purchases | 99,220 | |
| Creditors | | 4,050 |
| Rent Received | | 25,000 |
| Wages and Salaries | 32,000 | |
| Rates | 3,000 | |
| Bank overdraft | 2,550 | |
| Carriage Out | 2,350 | |
| Equipment | 70,000 | |
| Cash in Hand | 7,700 | |
| Issued Share Capital | | 40,000 |
| | 281,600 | 281,600 |

You are given the following information as at 31st December 2007:

(i) Closing Stock €19,000
(ii) Carriage In Due €770
(iii) Rent Received Due €3,000
(iv) Rates Due €350
(v) Carriage Out Due €1,880
(vi) Depreciation: Equipment 8%, Fixtures and Fittings 10%
(vii) Dividend Declared 18%

4. The following Trial Balance was extracted for the books of Ovington Sports Ltd on the 31st December 2001. The Authorised Share Capital is 500,000 IR£1 ordinary shares.
   You are required to prepare the company's Trading, Profit and Loss and Appropriation Accounts for the year ended 31st December 2001 and a Balance Sheet as at that date.

| | IR£ DR | IR£ CR |
|---|---|---|
| Sales | | 420,000 |
| Opening Stock | 47,500 | |
| Purchases | 230,000 | |
| Customs Duty | 1,050 | |
| Rent Received | | 40,950 |
| Sales Returns | 7,800 | |
| Advertising | 20,300 | |
| Vehicles | 85,000 | |
| Debtors | 53,650 | |
| Creditors | | 22,350 |
| Carriage Out | 14,700 | |
| Purchase Returns | | 9,700 |
| Wages | 68,000 | |
| Light and Heat | 9,800 | |
| Insurance | 10,200 | |
| Plant and Machinery | 100,000 | |
| Bank | 45,000 | |
| Issued Share Capital | | 200,000 |
| | 693,000 | 693,000 |

You are given the following information as at 31st December 2001:

(i) Closing Stock IR£40,000
(ii) Rent Received Prepaid IR£5,950
(iii) Insurance Due IR£800
(iv) Advertising Prepaid IR£3,300
(v) Depreciation: Plant and Machinery and Vehicles 12%
(vi) Dividend Declared 8%

5. The following Trial Balance was extracted for the books of Jones Oriental Arts Ltd on the 31st December 2004. The Authorised Share Capital is 150,000 €1 ordinary shares.
   You are required to prepare the company's Trading, Profit and Loss and Appropriation Accounts for the year ended 31st December 2004 and a Balance Sheet as at that date.

| | € DR | € CR |
|---|---|---|
| Sales | | 89,500 |
| Purchases | 43,000 | |
| Commission Received | | 7,000 |
| Opening Stock | 12,500 | |
| Carriage Out | 1,400 | |
| Sales Returns | 4,050 | |
| Premises | 70,000 | |
| Debtors | 3,000 | |
| Purchase Returns | | 3,500 |
| Interest Paid | 350 | |
| Light and Heat | 900 | |
| Carriage In | 4,450 | |
| Rent Received | | 800 |
| Wages | 8,000 | |
| Equipment | 30,000 | |
| Cash | 350 | |
| Creditors | | 4,520 |
| Bank Overdraft | | 2,680 |
| Issued Share Capital | | 70,000 |
| | 178,000 | 178,000 |

You are given the following information as at 31st December 2004:

(i) Closing Stock €13,500
(ii) Carriage In Due €120
(iii) Carriage Out Prepaid €70
(iv) Depreciation: Equipment 10%
(v) Dividend Declared 6%

## 1.7 ASSESSING THE PERFORMANCE OF A BUSINESS

The compilation of final accounts serves very little useful purpose other than meeting legal requirements. The following important factors are ignored in the final accounts:

- Staff morale, efficiency and experience
- Customer loyalty
- Asset values may be inaccurate, for example, premises may be undervalued
- The Balance Sheet is a financial statement that changes from day to day

It is important that the accounts are interpreted to find out certain information about the firm. The information that emerges is used to:

- Compare with previous results achieved by the business
- Compare with the results of other businesses in the same industry
- Compare with budget targets
- Assist in decision making and to take corrective action where appropriate.

The most common technique used to interpret financial accounts is known as **ratio analysis**. This information is of benefit to many interested parties.

### Interested Parties

- **Creditors** — They will examine the firm's ability to pay for goods supplied on credit.
- **Banks** — They are interested to determine the firm's ability to repay an overdraft and/or loan.
- **Shareholders and Investors** — They are interested in the firm's profit and subsequent dividends.
- **Management** — Compare the profit trends with previous years and with other businesses in the same sector. This aids the decision making process.
- **Employees/Trade Unions** — Job security at acceptable rates of pay is of prime importance.
- **Revenue Commissioners** — They ensure that the firm pays tax based on profits.

### Assessment Headings

The business may be assessed under the following headings using the appropriate ratios:

1. **Profitability Ratios**
   These measure how effective management are in the generation of profits
2. **Liquidity Ratios**
   These measure the firm's ability to meet its financial obligations as they fall due

3. **Solvency**
   A firm is solvent if its total assets are greater than its external liabilities
4. **Activity (Trade Performance) Ratios**
   These relate to the firm's activity, that is the speed at which the firm converts its current assets back into cash
5. **Dividend Policy**
   This is of most interest to the shareholder as management decides how much profit is given to shareholders in the form of rate of dividend

Each of the a[...]ing examples

Profitability Ratios
- Gross Margin
- Net Margin
- Gross Profit Make up
- Expenses to Sales Ratio
- Return on Capital Employed
- Return on Share Capital

***1. Profitability Ratios***

***Figure 1.4 — PROFITABILITY RATIOS [...]ement's efficiency in making profit***

| Gross Profit Percentage (Gross Margin) | Net Profit Percentage (Net Margin) |
|---|---|
| Gross Profit x 100 / Net Sales | Net Profit x 100 / Net Sales |

**Gross Profit Mark-Up**

*Gross Profit x 100*
*Cost of Sales*

**Expenses to Sales Ratio**

*Total Expenses x 100*
*Net Sales*

**Return on Capital Employed**

*Net Profit x 100*
*Capital Employed*

**Return on Share Capital**

*Net Profit x 100*
*Share Capital*

*Example*

Devlin Ltd produced final accounts for 1999 as set out below.

The Managing Director has asked you to assess the performance for the year under the heading of *profitability*.

| Trading, Profit and Loss and Appropriation Accounts for the year ended 31.7.99 | IR£ | IR£ |
|---|---|---|
| Sales | | 200,000 |
| Less cost of Sales | | 115,000 |
| Gross Profit | | 85,000 |
| Less Expenses | | 65,500 |
| Net Profit | | 19,500 |
| Less Dividends | | 2,500 |
| Reserves | | 17,000 |
| **Balance Sheet as at 31.7.99** | **IR£** | **IR£** |
| Fixed Assets | | 100,000 |
| Current Assets | 40,000 | |
| Less Current Liabilities | 30,000 | |
| Working Capital | | 10,000 |
| Total Net Assets | | 110,000 |
| Financed By: | | |
| Ordinary Share Capital | | 72,500 |
| Reserves | | 17,500 |
| Long Term Loan | | 20,000 |
| Capital Employed | | 110,000 |

SOLUTION

(a) Gross Profit Percentage (Gross Margin) = $\frac{\textit{Gross Profit} \times 100}{\textit{Net Sales}} = \frac{85{,}000 \times 100}{200{,}000} = 43\%$

This figure shows that 43 per cent (43p on each IR£1·00) of net sales remain as Gross Profit after having paid for the Cost of Sales but before accounting for the operating expenses of the business such as wages, light and heat, telephone etc.

(b) Net Profit Percentage (Net Margin) = $\frac{\textit{Net Profit} \times 100}{\textit{Net Sales}} = \frac{19{,}500 \times 100}{200{,}000} = 9{\cdot}75\%$

This figure shows that 9·75 per cent (9·75p on each IR£1·00) of net sales remain as Net Profit after having accounted for all of the expenses of the business.

(c) Gross Profit Mark-up = $\frac{\textit{Gross Profit} \times 100}{\textit{Cost of Sales}} = \frac{85{,}000 \times 100}{115{,}000} = 73{\cdot}9\%$

This figure shows that 73·9 per cent of the cost of goods sold contributes towards the Gross Profit. In other words a mark-up of 73·9 per cent is added to the cost of the goods in order to find the selling price (115,000 x 1·739 = 200,000).

(d) Expenses to Sales Ratio = $\frac{\textit{Total Expenses} \times 100}{\textit{Net Sales}} = \frac{65{,}500 \times 100}{200{,}000} = 32{\cdot}75\%$

This figure further investigates the Net Profit Percentage and shows that 32·75 per cent of net sales contribute towards the operating expenses of the business.

(e) Return on Capital Employed = $\frac{\textit{Net Profit} \times 100}{\textit{Capital Employed}} = \frac{19{,}500 \times 100}{110{,}000} = 17{\cdot}73\%$

This figure shows that Devlin Ltd has generated a return of 17·73 per cent on the capital employed or money invested in the business.

(f) Return on Share Capital = $\frac{\textit{Net Profit} \times 100}{\textit{Share Capital}} = \frac{19{,}500 \times 100}{72{,}500} = 26{\cdot}9\%$

This is one of the most beneficial ratios, particularly to shareholders, as they can compare the return made on his/her investment with other alternatives such as putting the funds in a deposit account in the bank.

**Note** *These figures indicate that Devlin Ltd is on a sound financial footing. However these may be best verified by comparing the results with the previous year's accounts or with another firm within the same industry. This allows all interested parties to identify particular trends and take appropriate action.*

## Practice Questions

1. Using the information supplied below calculate:
   *(i) Net Margin*
   *(ii) Gross margin*
   *(iii) Percentage Mark-up*
   *(iv) Expenses to Sales Ratio*

| Trading Account for year ending 31.9.99 | IR£ | IR£ |
|---|---|---|
| Sales | | 200,000 |
| Less cost of Sales | | 115,000 |
| Gross Profit | | 85,000 |
| Less Expenses | | 65,500 |
| Net Profit | | 19,500 |
| Less Dividends | | 2,500 |
| Reserves | | 17,000 |

2. Mr. Lysaght, a sole trader gave you the following figures:

| | |
|---|---|
| *Cost of Sales* | *IR£160,000* |
| *Sales* | *IR£200,000* |
| *Sales Returns* | *IR£10,000* |
| *Expenses* | *IR£20,000* |

Calculate:
*(a) The turnover for the period*
*(b) The Net Profit*
*(c) The Gross Profit Percentage*
*(d) The Net Profit Percentage*
*(e) The Expenses to Sales Ratio*

3. Doyle Ltd produced final accounts for 2000 as set out below.
The Managing Director has asked you to calculate the following:

| | |
|---|---|
| *(i) Gross Margin* | *(iv) Expenses to Sales Ratio* |
| *(ii Net Margin* | *(v) Return on Capital Employed* |
| *(iii) Gross Profit Mark-up* | *(vi) Return on Share Capital* |

| Trading, Profit and Loss and Appropriation Accounts for the year ended 31.12.00 | IR£ | IR£ |
|---|---|---|
| Sales | | 100,000 |
| Less cost of Sales | | 65,000 |
| Gross Profit | | 35,000 |
| Less Expenses | | 23,500 |
| Net Profit | | 11,500 |
| Less Dividends | | 1,500 |
| Reserves | | 10,000 |

| Balance Sheet as at 31.12.00 | IR£ | IR£ |
|---|---|---|
| Fixed Assets | | 80,000 |
| Current Assets | 30,000 | |
| Less Current Liabilities | 20,000 | |
| Working Capital | | 10,000 |
| Total Net Assets | | 90,000 |
| Financed By: | | |
| Ordinary Share Capital | | 50,000 |
| Reserves | | 10,000 |
| Long Term Loan | | 30,000 |
| Capital Employed | | 90,000 |

## 2. *Liquidity Ratios*

***Figure 1.5 — LIQUIDITY RATIOS (Measures the firm's ability to pay its short-term debts)***

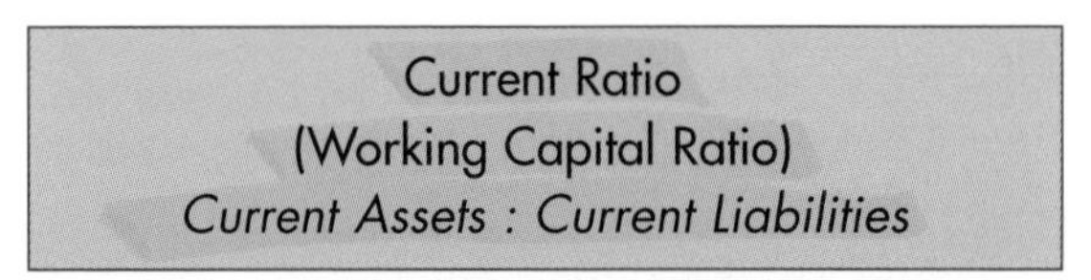


Acid Test Ratio
(Quick Ratio)
*Current Assets – Closing Stock : Current Liabilities*

***Example***

Using Devlin Ltd's Balance Sheet for the year ending 31.7.99, assess the performance for the year under the heading of *liquidity*.

**Note** Closing Stock at the year-end was IR£10,000.

| Balance Sheet as at 31.7.99 | IR£ | IR£ |
|---|---|---|
| Fixed Assets | | 100,000 |
| Current Assets | 40,000 | |
| Less Current Liabilities | 30,000 | |
| Working Capital | | 10,000 |
| Total Net Assets | | 110,000 |
| Financed By: | | |
| Ordinary Share Capital | | 72,500 |
| Reserves | | 17,500 |
| Long Term Loan | | 20,000 |
| Capital Employed | | 110,000 |

**SOLUTION**

(a) Current Ratio = *Current Assets : Current Liabilities*
(Working Capital Ratio) = 40,000 : 30,000
= 1·33 : 1

This figure shows that the firm is able to pay its short-term debts out of current assets. However it is below the recommended ratio of 2 : 1. This may give rise to problems such as:

1. Paying expenses which are incurred on a regular basis, for example, wages.
2. How to finance the company from the time of purchase of goods for resale to the time of subsequent sale.

To provide a more accurate ratio the acid test ratio (quick ratio) is used. This ratio omits the closing stock figure as it is generally accepted that it is the most difficult current asset to convert into cash. It is least liquid.

(b) Acid Test Ratio = *Current Assets – Closing Stock* : *Current Liabilities*
(Quick Ratio) = (40,000 - 10,000) : 30,000
= 30,000 : 30,000
= 1 : 1

This ratio equals the recommended ratio of 1 : 1. It can be concluded that Devlin Ltd is able to pay its current liabilities out of its most liquid current assets.

**Note** *Should the working capital be a negative figure, this indicates that the firm is* ***overtrading****. This problem arises as a result of too much money being tied up in stock and the amount owed to creditors is greater than money due from debtors.*

## Practice Questions

1. The following extract is taken from the Balance Sheet of Curry Ltd. You are asked to calculate and comment on:

   *(i) The Working Capital Ratio*
   *(ii) The Acid Test Ratio*

   The Closing Stock figure at the year-end was IR£15,000.

| Balance Sheet as at 31.7.99 | IR£ | IR£ |
|---|---|---|
| Fixed Assets | | 150,000 |
| Current Assets | 60,000 | |
| Less Current Liabilities | 40,000 | |
| Working Capital | | 20,000 |
| Total Net Assets | | 170,000 |

2. Using the balance sheet figures given in question 1 and a revised closing stock figure of IR£30,000 calculate the *Acid Test Ratio*. Comment on how the liquidity of the firm may be improved by making two suggestions.

3. A colleague with little knowledge of accounts has asked you to explain what is meant by *Working Capital* and *Overtrading*.

### *3. Solvency*

***Figure 1.6 — SOLVENCY (Determines whether the firm is solvent/insolvent (Bankrupt))***

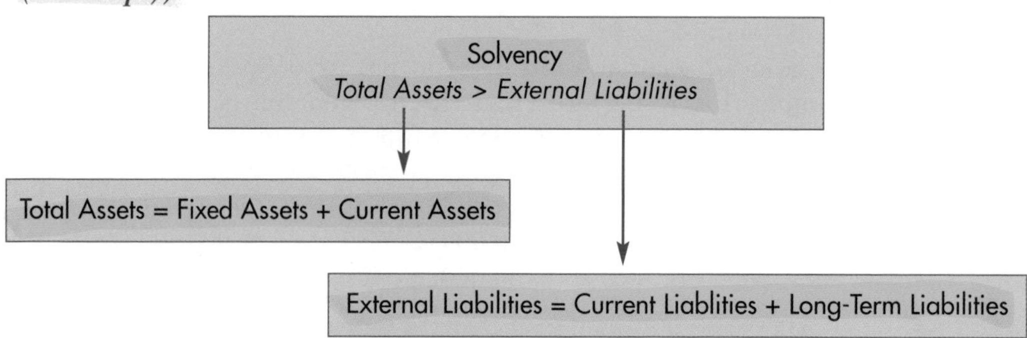


Should External Liabilities be greater than Total Assets the firm is said to be insolvent or bankrupt and should not continue to trade. If trading does continue the directors may be liable, under company law, to heavy penalties and may be prevented from being company directors in the future.

***Example***
Using Devlin Ltd's Balance Sheet for the year ended 31.7.99, determine whether or not the firm is solvent.

| **Balance Sheet as at 31.7.99** | **IR£** | **IR£** |
|---|---|---|
| Fixed Assets | | 100,000 |
| Current Assets | 40,000 | |
| Less Current Liabilities | 30,000 | |
| Working Capital | | 10,000 |
| Total Net Assets | | 110,000 |
| Financed By: | | |
| Ordinary Share Capital | | 72,500 |
| Reserves | | 17,500 |
| Long Term Loan | | 20,000 |
| Capital Employed | | 110,000 |

**SOLUTION**

| Solvency | = | Total Assets | exceeds | External Liabilities |
|---|---|---|---|---|
| | | (100,000 + 40,000) | > | (30,000 + 20,000) |
| | | 140,000 | > | 50,000 |

Therefore the firm is solvent. (Any firm that is insolvent must cease trading immediately)

### *4. Activity (Trade Performance) Ratios*

*Figure 1.7*

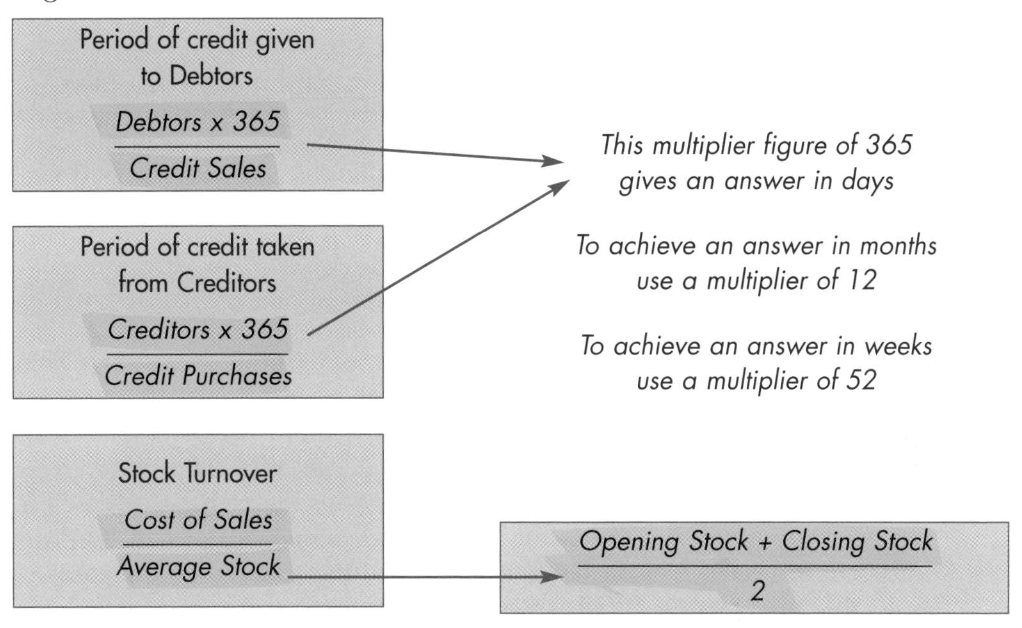


*Example*

| **Trading Account of O'Brien Ltd for the year ended 31.7.99** | **IR£** | **IR£** |
|---|---|---|
| Credit Sales | | 60,000 |
| Less Cost of Sales | | |
| Opening Stock | 3,600 | |
| Credit Purchases | 40,800 | |
| Cost of goods available for sale | 44,400 | |
| Less closing Stock | 4,400 | |
| Cost of Sales | | 40,000 |
| Gross Profit | | 20,000 |

**Note** At the year-end 31.7.99 the following is an extract taken from the Balance Sheet

| | |
|---|---|
| Debtors | IR£4,000 |
| Creditors | IR£2,040 |

You are required to calculate and comment on:

*(i) Average Stock*
*(ii) Stock Turnover*
*(iii) Period of credit given to debtors*
*(iv) Period of credit taken from creditors*

**Solution**

(a) Average Stock = $\frac{\textit{Opening Stock + Closing Stock}}{2} = \frac{3{,}600 + 4{,}400}{2}$ = IR£4000

This figure of IR£4000 is the average of the opening and closing stocks, and is used to calculate the stock turnover.

(b) Stock Turnover = $\frac{\textit{Cost of Sales}}{\textit{Average Stock}} = \frac{40{,}000}{4{,}000}$ = 10 times

This figure indicates that the average stock is sold 10 times in a year. This figure varies from one type of industry to another. *(For example, a newsagent would have a high rate of stock turnover whereas a jeweller would have a low stock turnover rate. However, the net profit percentage on sales of newspapers is considerably lower than that on sales of jewellery.)* If this figure has decreased it may show that sales are slowing down and some stock may become outdated and hard to sell. On the other hand if this figure increases it shows that the business carries lower levels of stocks and this may give rise to stock shortages.

(c) Period of Credit given to Debtors = $\frac{\textit{Debtors} \times 365}{\textit{Credit Sales}} = \frac{4{,}000 \times 365}{60{,}000}$ = 24·3 days

This figure indicates that the firm's debts are collected from the debtors, on average, every 24·3 days after the time of sale. This information is important as it shows the length of time that cash is tied up.

(d) Period of Credit taken from Creditors

$\frac{\textit{Creditors} \times 365}{\textit{Credit Purchases}} = \frac{2{,}040 \times 365}{40{,}800}$ = 18·2 days

This figure indicates that the firm pays its debts to the creditors, on average, every 18·2 days after the time of purchase. This information is important as it shows if the firm utilises the period of credit given by creditors. It should be monitored that the period of time given to debtors is not significantly greater than that taken from creditors.

## Exercises

1. Mr. James, a retailer gave you the following figures:

| | |
|---|---|
| *Cost of Sales* | *IR£160,000* |
| *Opening Stock* | *IR£20,000* |
| *Closing Stock* | *IR£10,000* |

Calculate: *(a) The Average Stock*
*(b) The Stock Turnover*

2.

| **Trading Account of Flood Ltd for the year ended 31.12.02** | **€** | **€** |
|---|---|---|
| Credit Sales | | 160,000 |
| Less Cost of Sales | | |
| Opening Stock | 13,000 | |
| Credit Purchases | 120,000 | |
| Cost of goods available for sale | 133,000 | |
| Less closing Stock | 11,000 | |
| Cost of Sales | | 122,000 |
| Gross Profit | | 38,000 |

**Note** At the year-end 31.12.02 the following is an extract taken from the Balance Sheet:

| | |
|---|---|
| Debtors | €8,000 |
| Creditors | €5,000 |

You are required to calculate and comment on:

*(a) Average Stock*
*(b) Stock Turnover*
*(c) Period of credit given to debtors*
*(d) Period of credit taken from creditors*

3.

| **Trading Account of McAree Ltd for the year ended 31.10.04** | **€** | **€** |
|---|---|---|
| Credit Sales | | 120,000 |
| Less Cost of Sales | | |
| Opening Stock | 7,000 | |
| Credit Purchases | 90,000 | |
| Cost of goods available for sale | 97,000 | |
| Less closing Stock | 5,000 | |
| Cost of Sales | | 92,000 |
| Gross Profit | | 28,000 |

**Note** At the year-end 31.10.04 the following is an extract taken from the Balance Sheet:

Debtors €12,000
Creditors €6,000

You are required to calculate and comment on:

*(a) Average Stock*
*(b) Stock Turnover*
*(c) Period of credit given to debtors in days, weeks and months*
*(d) Period of credit taken from creditors in days, weeks and months*

4.

| **Trading Account of McDonnell Ltd for the year ended 31.12.05** | **€** | **€** |
|---|---|---|
| Sales | | 100,000 |
| Less Cost of Sales | | |
| Gross Profit | | |
| Less Expenses | | |
| Net Profit | | |

(a) Given a Gross Profit Percentage of 35 per cent and a Net Margin Percentage of 20 per cent complete the above Trading Account.
(b) Average Stock is calculated to be €13,000. How many times per year is the average stock sold?

### 5. Dividend Policy

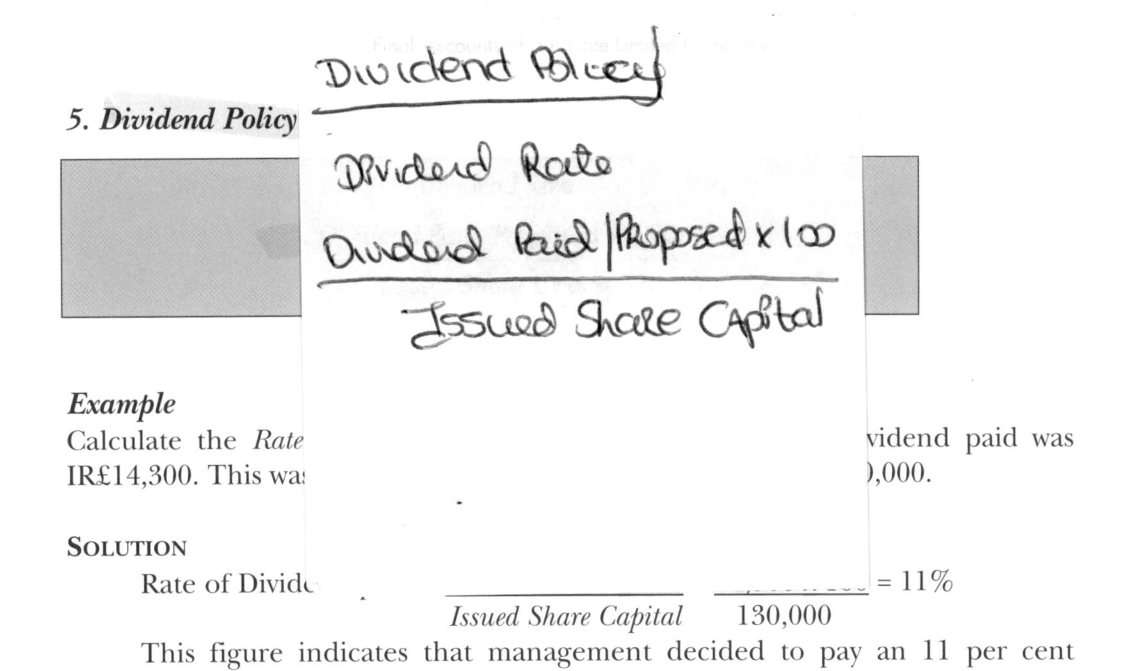


*Example*

Calculate the *Rate* ... vidend paid was IR£14,300. This wa ... ),000.

SOLUTION

Rate of Divid ... = 11%

*Issued Share Capital* 130,000

This figure indicates that management decided to pay an 11 per cent dividend to shareholders.

## Practice Questions

Calculate the rate of dividend paid from the information provided in the following questions:

1. *Dividend Paid* — *IR£10,000*
   *Authorised Share Capital* — *IR£150,000*
   *Issued Share Capital* — *IR£100,000*

2. *Dividend Paid* — *IR£7,500*
   *Authorised Share Capital* — *IR£100,000*
   *Issued Share Capital* — *IR£60,000*

3. *Dividend Paid* — *IR£10,800*
   *Authorised Share Capital* — *IR£200,000*
   *Issued Share Capital* — *IR£180,000*

## Comprehensive Example

Examine the Final Accounts and Balance Sheets of Buz Ltd, set out below, for the years 1995 and 1996. Compare and comment on the performance of the company for the two years using the following ratios:

*(i)* *Gross Profit Margin*
*(ii)* *Return on Capital Employed*
*(iii)* *Acid Test (Quick) Ratio*
*(iv)* *Rate of Dividend Paid*

Show all your workings.
(Junior Certificate Higher Level 1997 PII Q4(b))

| 1995 Trading, Profit and Loss and Appropriation Accounts for the year ended 31.5.95 | | | 1996 Trading, Profit and Loss and Appropriation Accounts for the year ended 31.5.96 | | |
|---|---|---|---|---|---|
| | | IR£ | | | IR£ |
| Sales | | 190,000 | Sales | | 230,000 |
| Gross Profit | | 75,000 | Gross Profit | | 82,000 |
| Net Profit | | 43,000 | Net Profit | | 55,000 |
| Dividends Paid | | 14,300 | Dividends Paid | | 16,900 |
| Reserves | | 28,700 | Reserves | | 38,100 |
| **Balance Sheet as at 31.5.95** | | | **Balance Sheet as at 31.5.96** | | |
| | IR£ | IR£ | | IR£ | |
| Fixed Assets | | 180,000 | Fixed Assets | | 198,000 |
| Current Assets (Including Closing Stock IR£7,000) | 25,700 | | Current Assets (Including Closing Stock IR£5,300) | 36,800 | |
| Less Current Liabilities | 17,000 | 8,700 | Less Current Liabilities | 18,000 | 18,800 |
| | | 188,700 | | | 216,800 |
| Financed By | | | Financed By | | |
| 130,000 IR£1 Ordinary Shares | | 130,000 | 130,000 IR£1 Ordinary Shares | | 130,000 |
| Reserves | | 28,700 | Reserves | | 66,800 |
| Long-term Liabilities | | 30,000 | Long-term Liabilities | | 20,000 |
| | | 188,700 | | | 216,800 |

**SOLUTION**

(i) Gross Profit Margin

| | 1995 | 1996 |
|---|---|---|
| $\frac{\textit{Gross Profit} \times 100}{\textit{Sales}}$ | $\frac{75{,}000 \times 100}{190{,}000}$ = 39·47% | $\frac{82{,}000 \times 100}{230{,}000}$ = 35·65% |

The Gross Profit Margin has decreased by almost 10 per cent in 1996. Even though Gross Profit and Sales have increased in 1996 this drop may be attributed to an increase in the cost of sales.

(ii) Return on Capital Employed

| | 1995 | 1996 |
|---|---|---|
| *Net Profit* x *100* / *Capital Employed* | 43,000 x 100 / 188,700 = 22·79% | 55,000 x 100 / 216,800 = 25·37% |

The Return on Capital Employed has increased by 11.32 per cent. This shows that management has been more efficient in using the capital employed to make profits in 1996. This figure compares favourably to the return that would be earned if the funds where invested elsewhere.

(iii) Acid Test (Quick Ratio)

| | 1995 | 1996 |
|---|---|---|
| *Current Assets – Closing Stock : Current Liabilities* | (25,700 – 7,000) : 17,000 = 18,700 : 17,000 = 1·1 : 1 | (36,800 – 5,300) : 18,000 = 31,500 : 18,000 = 1·75 : 1 |

The Acid Test ratio in 1995 is close to the recommended average of 1:1. The figure for 1996 is higher and this shows that Buz Ltd has IR£1·75 of current assets (excluding closing stock) available to pay for each IR£1 of current liabilities.

(iv) Rate of Dividend Paid

| | 1995 | 1996 |
|---|---|---|
| *Dividend Paid* x *100* / *Issued Share Capital* | 14,300 x 100 / 130,000 = 11% | 16,900 x 100 / 130,000 = 13% |

These figures are of most interest to the shareholders of Buz Ltd. This shows that the capital invested by them is earning a higher return in 1996. This return is much greater than the return offered, for example, by banks if his/her funds were on deposit.

Overall Buz Ltd has produced a strong set of accounts for both years. However, it is clear that the company has grown in 1996 and the management should consider the possibility of ploughing some of the reserves back into the business in order to maintain and build upon this success.

## Practice Questions

1. The Final Accounts and Balance Sheets of ABC Ltd are set out below for the years 1999 and 2000.

   You are required to calculate for both years:

   (a) Net Margin
   (b) Gross Margin
   (c) Gross Profit Mark-up
   (d) Expenses to Sales Ratio
   (e) Return on Capital Employed
   (f) Return on Share Capital
   (g) Current Ratio
   (h) Quick Ratio
   (i) Average Stock
   (j) Stock Turnover
   (k) Period of Credit given to Debtors
   (l) Period of Credit taken from Creditors
   (m) Dividend Rate

| **1999** **Trading, Profit and Loss and Appropriation Accounts of ABC Ltd for the year ended 31.12.99** | | **2000** **Trading, Profit and Loss and Appropriation Accounts of ABC Ltd for the year ended 31.12.00** | |
|---|---|---|---|
| | **IR£** | | **IR£** |
| Credit Sales | 100,000 | Credit Sales | 150,000 |
| Less Cost of Sales | 60,000 | Less Cost of Sales | 110,000 |
| Gross Profit | 40,000 | Gross Profit | 40,000 |
| Less Expenses | 25,000 | Less Expenses | 30,000 |
| Net Profit | 15,000 | Net Profit | 10,000 |
| Less Dividends Paid | 5,000 | Less Dividends Paid | 4,000 |
| Reserves | 10,000 | Reserves | 6,000 |

| **Balance Sheet as at 31.12.99** | | | **Balance Sheet as at 31.12.00** | | |
|---|---|---|---|---|---|
| | **IR£** | **IR£** | | **IR£** | **IR£** |
| Fixed Assets | | 100,000 | Fixed Assets | | 100,000 |
| Current Assets | 60,000 | | Current Assets | 50,000 | |
| Less Current Liabilities | 30,000 | 30,000 | Less Current Liabilities | 20,000 | 30,000 |
| | | 130,000 | | | 130,000 |
| Financed By | | | Financed By | | |
| Ordinary Share Capital | | 80,000 | Ordinary Share Capital | | 80,000 |
| Reserves | | 10,000 | Reserves | | 16,000 |
| Long-term Liabilities | | 40,000 | Long-term Liabilities | | 34,000 |
| | | 130,000 | | | 130,000 |

The following additional information is provided:

| | *1999* | *2000* |
|---|---|---|
| *Opening Stock* | *IR£4,000* | *IR£5,000* |
| *Closing Stock* | *IR£3,000* | *IR£5,000* |
| *Debtors* | *IR£10,000* | *IR£14,000* |
| *Creditors* | *IR£7,000* | *IR£12,500* |
| *Credit Purchases* | *IR£59,000* | *IR£110,000* |

2. Examine the Final Accounts and Balance Sheets of King Ltd, set out below, for the years 1993 and 1994. Compare and comment on the performance of the company for the two years using the following headings. Show all your workings.

   *(i) Profitability*
   *(ii) Liquidity*
   *(iii) Dividend Policy*

   (Adapted from Junior Certificate Higher Level 1994 PII Q5)

| **1993 Trading, Profit and Loss and Appropriation Accounts for the year ended 31.5.93** | | **1994 Trading, Profit and Loss and Appropriation Accounts for the year ended 31.5.94** | |
|---|---|---|---|
| | **IR£** | | **IR£** |
| Sales | 140,000 | Sales | 270,000 |
| Less Cost of Sales | 84,000 | Less Cost of Sales | 108,000 |
| Gross Profit | 56,000 | Gross Profit | 162,000 |
| Less Expenses | 44,600 | Less Expenses | 133,500 |
| Net Profit | 11,400 | Net Profit | 28,500 |
| Less Dividends | 1,400 | Less Dividends | 10,500 |
| Reserves | 10,000 | Reserves | 18,000 |

| Balance Sheet as at 31.5.93 | | | Balance Sheet as at 31.5.94 | | |
|---|---|---|---|---|---|
| | IR£ | IR£ | | IR£ | IR£ |
| Fixed Assets | | 105,000 | Fixed Assets | | 95,000 |
| Current Assets | 20,000 | | Current Assets | 30,000 | |
| Less Current Liabilities | 30,000 | (10,000) | Less Current Liabilities | 15,000 | 15,000 |
| | | 95,000 | | | 110,000 |
| Financed By | | | Financed By | | |
| Ordinary Share Capital | | 70,000 | Ordinary Share Capital | | 70,000 |
| Reserves | | 10,000 | Reserves | | 28,000 |
| Long-term Liabilities | | 15,000 | Long-term Liabilities | | 12,000 |
| | | 95,000 | | | 110,000 |

3. Hido Ltd has an Authorised Share Capital of 150,000 IR£1 Ordinary Shares. It supplies you with the following information for the year ended 31.5.92:

| | | | |
|---|---|---|---|
| *Sales* | *IR£200,000* | *Expenses* | *IR£60,000* |
| *Cost of Sales* | *IR£80,000* | *Issued Share Capital* | *IR£120,000* |
| *Capital Employed* | *IR£240,000* | *Closing Stock* | *IR£15,000* |
| *Debtors* | *IR£20,000* | *Dividends Declared* | *20%* |
| *Current Liabilities* | *IR£20,000* | | |

Calculate the following:

*(i)* *The gross Profit Margin*
*(ii)* *The Return on Capital Employed*
*(iii)* *The amount of extra capital Hido Ltd can raise from issuing shares*
*(iv)* *The profit retained by Hido Ltd at 31.5.92*
*(v)* *The amount Hido Ltd had in the bank if the current ratio was 2:1*
*(vi)* *You own 6,000 shares in Hido Ltd. How much will you receive in the form of dividends?*

(Adapted from Junior Certificate Higher Level 1992 PII Q6)

# CHAPTER 2
# DOUBLE-ENTRY BOOKKEEPING

Double-entry bookkeeping is used to record the financial transactions of a business in an organised way so that the business has an accurate record of its transactions.

## 2.1 RULES FOR DOUBLE-ENTRY BOOKKEEPING

This is based on the rule that every financial transaction has two parts. The business gives and someone else receives or someone gives and the business receives.

***THE FIRST SKILL YOU REQUIRE IS THE ABILITY TO IDENTIFY THE TWO ACCOUNTS INVOLVED IN EACH TRANSACTION.***

### *Examples*

*Purchased Premises for IR£20,000, paid by Cheque*

➘ The two accounts are Premises Account and Bank Account

*Paid ESB bill in full, IR£250 by cash*

➘ The two accounts are ESB Account and Cash Account

**Note** All FIXED ASSETS are recorded in an account named after the asset e.g. Premises Account, Machinery Account, Vehicle Account etc.
All EXPENSES are recorded in an account named after the expense e.g. Wages Account, Insurance Account, Telephone Account etc.

### *Worked Example*

Boyd Ltd has just been incorporated and its first transactions are examined below, note that each transaction involves two accounts.

| Transactions | Accounts Involved | |
|---|---|---|
| Issued 150,000 IR£1 **Ordinary shares,** money was **lodged** | Share Capital a/c | Bank a/c |
| Purchased **premises** for IR£90,000 by **cheque** | Premises a/c | Bank a/c |
| **Purchased goods** for IR£5,000, paid by **cheque** | Purchases a/c | Bank a/c |
| **Sold goods** for **cash** IR£3,000 | Sales a/c | Cash a/c |
| **Sold goods** on **credit to Coxy Ltd** for IR£1,500 | Sales a/c | Coxy Ltd a/c |
| Paid **wages** in **cash** IR£1,000 | Wages a/c | Cash a/c |

| Transactions *contd.* | Accounts Involved *contd.* | |
|---|---|---|
| **Coxy Ltd — returned faulty goods** worth IR£200 | Coxy Ltd a/c | Sales Returns a/c |
| **Bought goods on credit from Jones Ltd** IR£1,600 | Purchases a/c | Jones Ltd a/c |
| **Coxy Ltd** paid IR£1,300, money was **lodged** | Coxy Ltd a/c | Bank a/c |
| Paid **Jones Ltd** IR£1,600 by **cheque** | Jones Ltd a/c | Bank a/c |

There is much we can learn from the transactions of Boyd Ltd. We can identify accounts from key words. All goods sold are recorded in the Sales Account. All goods purchased are recorded in the Purchases Account. All fixed assets are recorded in an account named after the fixed asset. All expenses are recorded in an account named after the expense. The use of 'by cheque' or 'lodged' indicates bank transactions.

## Credit Transactions

There are a special group of transactions which take place 'ON CREDIT'. These are transactions where no payment is made until sometime in the future. The buyer of goods promises to pay at a later date. It is important that a business keeps a record of money that is owed (to it and by it) because of these transactions.

The accounts for credit transactions are as follows:

*Selling on credit* ........................................ *Sales a/c and Debtors a/c*
*Buying on credit* ........................................ *Purchases a/c and Creditors a/c*
*Returning goods to a creditor* ...................... *Purchase Returns a/c and Creditors a/c*
*Goods returned by a debtor* .......................... *Sales Returns a/c and Debtors a/c*
*Pay a creditor by cheque* .............................. *Bank a/c and Creditors a/c*
*Receive payment (lodged) from a debtor* ........ *Bank a/c and Debtors a/c*

The Debtors' and Creditors' Accounts above are named according to the name of the debtor or creditor (i.e. Coxy Ltd Account, where Coxy Ltd is the debtor or Jones Ltd Account, where Jones Ltd is the creditor).

## Rules for Account Entries

There are two sets of rules you can use to enter transactions into their relevant accounts. First we must look at what an account looks like. As the name Double Entry suggests, each account has two sides. The left hand side is called the Debit Side and the right hand side is called the Credit Side. We call this type of account a 'T-Account'.

Both sides of the account record information in a similar manner.

- The debit side records that part of the transaction that is received by the business, e.g. money paid to the business, purchases made by the business etc.

► The credit side records that part of the transaction given by the business, e.g. shares issued by the business, sales made by the business etc.

*Figure 2.1 — Layout of a T-Account*

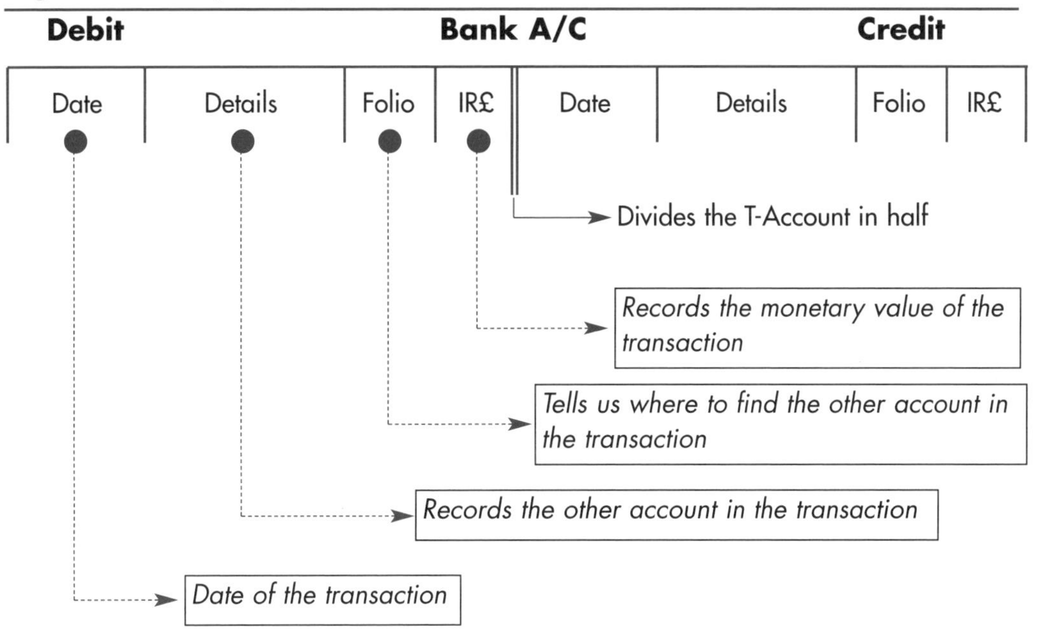


***THE SECOND SKILL YOU REQUIRE IS THE ABILITY ENTER INFORMATION ON THE CORRECT SIDE OF AN ACCOUNT. THERE ARE TWO SETS OF RULES FOR THIS:***

*Rule 1*

***'DEBIT THE RECEIVER AND CREDIT THE GIVER'***

This rule recognises that in each transaction there is something given and something received.

***Examples***

*Purchased Premises for IR£20,000, paid by Cheque*

- Debit Premises Account and Credit Bank Account
- The business receives premises — in return it gives IR£20,000

*Paid ESB bill in full, IR£250 by cash*

- Debit ESB Account and Credit Cash Account
- The business has received electricity worth IR£250 — for which it pays in cash

*Tip:*

Sometimes it is hard to see which account is giving and which is receiving. But you should always be able to work out one or the other. If you know one account is a debit, then the other account must be a credit and vice versa.

***'For every debit there is a corresponding credit and vice versa'***

*Example*

Boyd Ltd has just been incorporated and its first transactions are examined below, note that each transaction involves two accounts.

| Transactions | Accounts Involved | |
|---|---|---|
| Issued 150,000 IR£1 Ordinary shares, money was lodged | **CR** Share Capital a/c | **DR** Bank a/c |
| Purchased premises for IR£90,000 by cheque | **DR** Premises a/c | **CR** Bank a/c |
| Purchased goods for IR£5,000, paid by cheque | **DR** Purchases a/c | **CR** Bank a/c |
| Sold goods for cash IR£3,000 | **CR** Sales a/c | **DR** Cash a/c |
| Sold goods on credit to Coxy Ltd for IR£1,500 | **CR** Sales a/c | **DR** Coxy Ltd a/c |
| Paid wages in cash IR£1,000 | **DR** Wages a/c | **CR** Cash a/c |
| Coxy Ltd — returned faulty goods worth IR£200 | **CR** Coxy Ltd a/c | **DR** Sales Returns a/c |
| Bought goods on credit from Jones Ltd IR£1,600 | **DR** Purchases a/c | **CR** Jones Ltd a/c |
| Coxy Ltd paid IR£1,300, money was lodged | **CR** Coxy Ltd a/c | **DR** Bank a/c |
| Paid Jones Ltd IR£1,600 by cheque | **DR** Jones Ltd a/c | **CR** Bank a/c |

Where DR = Debit and CR = Credit

*Rule 2*

This rule is more complex but it can be applied all the way up to Leaving Certificate Accounting. There are two parts to it:

Firstly you must establish whether the transaction caused an increase or a decrease in the monetary value of an account. We will use '+' to denote an increase in monetary value and '–' to denote a decrease in the monetary value.

Secondly you must establish whether each of the two accounts involved in the transaction is an asset, liability, revenue or expense. An asset is something owned by a business, e.g. premises, equipment, cash etc. A liability is something owed by the business, e.g. creditors, bank overdraft etc. A revenue is income earned by the business, e.g. sales, rent received etc. An expense is a cost incurred in running the business, e.g. purchases, rent etc.

*Debit Entries*

In the case of an asset or expense account, all increases (+) in value are debited. In the case of a liability account, all decreases (–) in value are debited.

*Credit Entries*

In the case of an asset or expense account, all decreases (–) in value are credited. In the case of a revenue account, all increases (+) in value are credited.

*Example*

Boyd Ltd has just been incorporated and its first transactions are examined below, note that each transaction involves two accounts.

| Transactions | Accounts Involved | |
|---|---|---|
| Issued 150,000 IR£1 Ordinary shares, money was lodged | *Share Capital a/c*<br>**+L therefore CR** | *Bank a/c*<br>**+A therefore DR** |
| Purchased premises for IR£90,000 by cheque | *Premises a/c*<br>**+A therefore DR** | *Bank a/c*<br>**-A therefore CR** |
| Purchased goods for IR£5,000, paid by cheque | *Purchases a/c*<br>**-E therefore DR** | *Bank a/c*<br>**-A therefore CR** |
| Sold goods for cash IR£3,000 | *Sales a/c*<br>**+R therefore CR** | *Cash a/c*<br>**+A therefore DR** |
| Sold goods on credit to Coxy Ltd for IR£1,500 | *Sales a/c*<br>**+R therefore CR** | *Coxy Ltd a/c*<br>**+A therefore DR** |
| Paid wages in cash IR£1,000 | *Wages a/c*<br>**+E therefore DR** | *Cash a/c*<br>**-A therefore CR** |
| Coxy Ltd — returned faulty goods worth IR£200 | *Coxy Ltd a/c*<br>**-A therefore CR** | *Sales Returns a/c*<br>**+E therefore DR** |
| Bought goods on credit from Jones Ltd IR£1,600 | *Purchases a/c*<br>**+E therefore DR** | *Jones Ltd a/c*<br>**+L therefore CR** |
| Coxy Ltd paid IR£1,300, money was lodged | *Coxy Ltd a/c*<br>**-A therefore CR** | *Bank a/c*<br>**+A therefore DR** |
| Paid Jones Ltd IR£1,600 by cheque | *Jones Ltd a/c*<br>**-L therefore DR** | *Bank a/c*<br>**-A therefore CR** |

*Where:*
*'+' denotes an increase in monetary value*
*'–' denotes a decrease in monetary value*
*'A' denotes an asset*
*'L' denotes a liability*
*'R' denotes a revenue*
*'E' denotes an expense*
*'DR' denotes Debit*
*'CR' denotes Credit*

These rules for debiting and crediting an account are often best understood when presented in the form of a T-Account, as follows:

*Figure 2.2 — Summary of Rules for Debiting and Crediting Accounts*

| DR | ASSET ACCOUNT | CR |
|---|---|---|
| + Records an increase in the monetary value of an asset | Records a decrease in the monetary value of an asset | − |

| DR | LIABILITY ACCOUNT | CR |
|---|---|---|
| − Records a decrease in the monetary value of a liability | Records an increase in the monetary value of a liability | + |

| DR | REVENUE ACCOUNT | CR |
|---|---|---|
| | Records revenue earned by the business | + |

| DR | EXPENSE ACCOUNT | CR |
|---|---|---|
| + Records expenses incurred by the business | | |

***Worked Example***

Boyd Ltd has just been incorporated, record these transactions in the correct accounts.

| | |
|---|---|
| 1 Jan | Issued 150,000 IR£1 Ordinary shares, money was lodged |
| 2 Jan | Purchased premises for IR£90,000 by cheque |
| 3 Jan | Purchased goods for IR£5,000, paid by cheque |
| 5 Jan | Sold goods for cash IR£3,000 |
| 7 Jan | Sold goods on credit to Coxy Ltd for IR£1,500 |
| 7 Jan | Paid wages in cash IR£1,000 |
| 8 Jan | Coxy Ltd — returned faulty goods worth IR£200 |
| 8 Jan | Bought goods on credit from Jones Ltd R£1,600 |
| 9 Jan | Coxy Ltd paid IR£1,300, money was lodged |
| 9 Jan | Paid Jones Ltd IR£1,600 by cheque |

**The Books of Boyd Ltd for January**

| DR | | | Bank Account (1) | | | | CR |
|---|---|---|---|---|---|---|---|
| 1 Jan | Share Capital | 2 | 150,000 | 2 Jan | Premises | 3 | 90,000 |
| 9 Jan | Coxy Ltd | 7 | 1,300 | 3 Jan | Purchases | 4 | 5,000 |
| | | | | 9 Jan | Jones Ltd | 10 | 1,600 |

| DR | | | Share Capital Account (2) | | | | CR |
|---|---|---|---|---|---|---|---|
| | | | | 1 Jan | Bank | 1 | 150,000 |

| DR | | Premises Account (3) | | | | | CR |
|---|---|---|---|---|---|---|---|
| 2 Jan | Bank | 1 | 90,000 | | | | |

| DR | | Purchases Account (4) | | | | | CR |
|---|---|---|---|---|---|---|---|
| 3 Jan | Bank | 1 | 5,000 | | | | |
| 8 Jan | Jones Ltd | 10 | 1,600 | | | | |

| DR | | Sales Account (5) | | | | | CR |
|---|---|---|---|---|---|---|---|
| | | | | 5 Jan | Cash | 6 | 3,000 |
| | | | | 7 Jan | Coxy Ltd | 7 | 1,500 |

| DR | | Cash Account (6) | | | | | CR |
|---|---|---|---|---|---|---|---|
| 5 Jan | Sales | 5 | 3,000 | 7 Jan | Wages | 8 | 1,000 |

| DR | | Coxy Ltd Account (7) | | | | | CR |
|---|---|---|---|---|---|---|---|
| 7 Jan | Credit Sales | 5 | 1,500 | 8 Jan | Sales Returns | 9 | 200 |
| | | | | 9 Jan | Bank | 1 | 1,300 |

| DR | | Wages Account (8) | | | | | CR |
|---|---|---|---|---|---|---|---|
| 7 Jan | Cash | 6 | 1,000 | | | | |

| DR | | Sales Returns Account (9) | | | | | CR |
|---|---|---|---|---|---|---|---|
| 8 Jan | Coxy Ltd | 7 | 200 | | | | |

| DR | | Jones Ltd Account (10) | | | | | CR |
|---|---|---|---|---|---|---|---|
| 9 Jan | Bank | 1 | 1,600 | 8 Jan | Credit Purchases | 4 | 1,600 |

**Notes** The first column on each side is the date, the second are the details, the third the folio and the last the monetary value of the transaction.

Each account has been given a number, these numbers represent page numbers. In real life the account would be spread throughout a whole book, so page numbers will tell you where to find the other account involved in the transaction.

The numbers in the folio columns relate to the page number for the other account involved in the transaction.

## 2.2 BALANCING A T-ACCOUNT

Now we have the transactions entered in the accounts we have to balance the accounts. This process gives us important information such as how much money is left in the business bank account, the value of our sales, wages paid, debts outstanding from debtors and to creditors.

Balancing is the method used to find out how much is left in an account, it also closes off the account at a certain date and opens it again at the start of the next accounting period.

### Method

1. Total (add up) both sides of the account.
2. Subtract the smaller total from the larger one.
3. The difference (answer to 2 above) is called the Balance Carried Down (Balance c/d) and is entered on the smaller side of the account.
4. Once again total both sides of the account, both sides should now be equal.
5. Enter the Balance c/d on the larger side of the account below the totals, now it's called the Balance Brought Down (Balance b/d).
6. Draw a double line under the totals on each side, this shows that the information above the totals is finished with.

***Note*** *If there is only one entry in an account it is not necessary to balance the account, that one entry is in effect the balance brought down.*

*Example A*

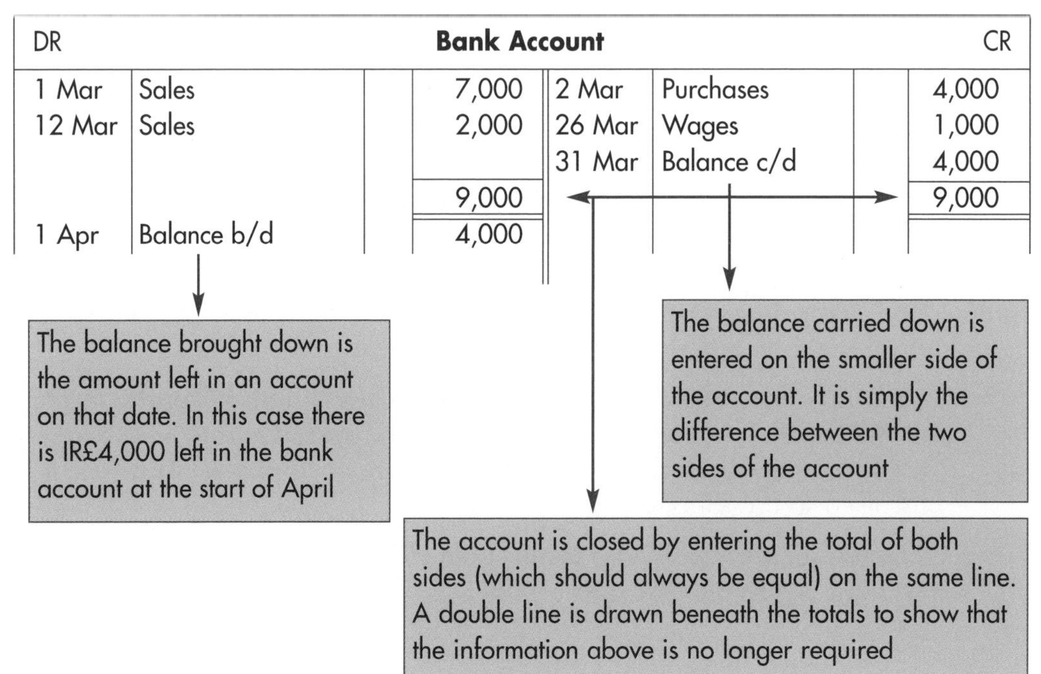

| DR | | Bank Account | | | | | CR |
|---|---|---|---|---|---|---|---|
| 1 Mar | Sales | | 7,000 | 2 Mar | Purchases | | 4,000 |
| 12 Mar | Sales | | 2,000 | 26 Mar | Wages | | 1,000 |
| | | | | 31 Mar | Balance c/d | | 4,000 |
| | | | 9,000 | | | | 9,000 |
| 1 Apr | Balance b/d | | 4,000 | | | | |

*Example B*

| DR | | Sludds Ltd | | | | | CR |
|---|---|---|---|---|---|---|---|
| 8 Jan | Bank | | 2,000 | 1 Jan | Balance b/d | | 2,000 |
| | | | | 10 Jan | Purchases | | 4,000 |
| 31 Jan | Balance c/d | | 6,000 | 22 Jan | Purchases | | 2,000 |
| | | | 8,000 | | | | 8,000 |
| | | | | 1 Feb | Balance b/d | | 6,000 |

**Notes**

1. In this account there is a Balance b/d on 1st January. This shows a balance from the previous month. In this case, Sludds Ltd is owed IR£2,000 from the previous month.
2. The balancing at the end of January is completed in the same manner as above except in this case the debit side has the smaller monetary value
3. On the 1st February Sludds Ltd is owed IR£6,000

**The Books of Boyd Ltd for January**

| DR | | Bank Account (1) | | | | | CR |
|---|---|---|---|---|---|---|---|
| 1 Jan | Share Capital | 2 | 150,000 | 2 Jan | Premises | 3 | 90,000 |
| 9 Jan | Coxy Ltd | 7 | 1,300 | 3 Jan | Purchases | 4 | 5,000 |
| | | | | 9 Jan | Jones Ltd | 10 | 1,600 |
| | | | | 31 Jan | Balance c/d | | 54,700 |
| | | | 151,300 | | | | 151,300 |
| 1 Feb | Balance b/d | | 54,700 | | | | |

| DR | | Share Capital Account (2) | | | | | CR |
|---|---|---|---|---|---|---|---|
| | | | | 1 Jan | Bank | 1 | 150,000 |

| DR | | Premises Account (3) | | | | | CR |
|---|---|---|---|---|---|---|---|
| 2 Jan | Bank | 1 | 90,000 | | | | |

| DR | | Purchases Account (4) | | | | | CR |
|---|---|---|---|---|---|---|---|
| 3 Jan | Bank | 1 | 5,000 | | | | |
| 8 Jan | Jones Ltd | 10 | 1,600 | 31 Jan | Balance c/d | | 6,600 |
| | | | 6,600 | | | | 6,600 |
| 1 Feb | Balance b/d | | 6,600 | | | | |

| DR | | | Sales Account (5) | | | | CR |
|---|---|---|---|---|---|---|---|
| | | | | 5 Jan | Cash | 6 | 3,000 |
| 31 Jan | Balance c/d | | 4,500 | 7 Jan | Coxy Ltd | 7 | 1,500 |
| | | | 4,500 | | | | 4,500 |
| | | | | 1 Feb | Balance b/d | | 4,500 |

| DR | | | Cash Account (6) | | | | CR |
|---|---|---|---|---|---|---|---|
| 5 Jan | Sales | 5 | 3,000 | 7 Jan | Wages | 8 | 1,000 |
| | | | | 31 Jan | Balance c/d | | 2,000 |
| | | | 3,000 | | | | 3,000 |
| 1 Feb | Balance b/d | | 2,000 | | | | |

| DR | | | Coxy Ltd Account (7) | | | | CR |
|---|---|---|---|---|---|---|---|
| 7 Jan | Credit Sales | 5 | 1,500 | 8 Jan | Sales Returns | 9 | 200 |
| | | | | 9 Jan | Bank | 1 | 1,300 |
| | | | 1,500 | | | | 1,500 |

| DR | | | Wages Account (8) | | | | CR |
|---|---|---|---|---|---|---|---|
| 7 Jan | Cash | 6 | 1,000 | | | | |

| DR | | | Sales Returns Account (9) | | | | CR |
|---|---|---|---|---|---|---|---|
| 8 Jan | Coxy Ltd | 7 | 200 | | | | |

| DR | | | Jones Ltd Account (10) | | | | CR |
|---|---|---|---|---|---|---|---|
| 9 Jan | Bank | 1 | 1,600 | 8 Jan | Credit Purchases | 4 | 1,600 |

## Practice Questions

Balance the following T-Accounts:

1.

| DR | | | Purchases Account | | | | CR |
|---|---|---|---|---|---|---|---|
| 1.5.02 | Bank | CB | 1,200 | | | | |
| 7.5.02 | Archer Ltd | CL | 1,700 | | | | |
| 15.5.02 | Smith Ltd | CL | 2,100 | | | | |
| | | | | | | | |
| | | | | | | | |
| | | | | | | | |

2.

| DR | | | VAT Account | | | | CR |
|---|---|---|---|---|---|---|---|
| 6.3.04 | Credit Purchases | PDB | 4,050 | 14.3.04 | Cash Sales | CB | 4,000 |
| 7.3.04 | Cash Purchases | CB | 3,500 | 17.3.04 | Credit Sales | SDB | 7,000 |
| | | | | | | | |
| | | | | | | | |
| | | | | | | | |
| | | | | | | | |

3.

| DR | | | King Ltd Account | | | | CR |
|---|---|---|---|---|---|---|---|
| 11.4.03 | Bank | CB | 40,000 | 1.4.03 | Balance | GJ | 24,000 |
| | | | | 7.4.03 | Credit Purchases | PDB | 37,030 |
| | | | | 17.4.03 | Credit Purchases | PDB | 21,700 |
| | | | | | | | |
| | | | | | | | |

4.

| DR | | | Adams Ltd Account | | | | CR |
|---|---|---|---|---|---|---|---|
| 1.11.99 | Balance | GJ | 17,330 | 4.11.99 | Bank | CB | 30,500 |
| 7.11.99 | Credit Sales | SDB | 21,000 | | | | |
| | | | | | | | |
| | | | | | | | |
| | | | | | | | |

5.

| DR | | | VAT Account | | | | CR |
|---|---|---|---|---|---|---|---|
| 1.12.01 | Credit Purchases | PDB | 20,500 | 4.12.01 | Cash Sales | CB | 7,770 |
| | | | | 9.12.01 | Credit Sales | SDB | 10,300 |
| | | | | | | | |
| | | | | | | | |
| | | | | | | | |

## 2.3 TRIAL BALANCE

A trial balance is simply a list of all the Debit and Credit balances brought down on a particular date. An account with only one entry is not usually balanced. The amount in such an account is entered straight into the trial balance. The balance amount is entered on the same side in the Trial Balance as it is in the account. Both the debit and credit columns are totalled up, they should be equal.

### Purpose

The trial balance acts as a check on the accuracy of our double-entry book-keeping. If the trial balance does not balance the Bookkeeper is alerted to search for errors within the accounts or in the trial balance itself.

It should be noted that unfortunately not all errors will affect the trial balance. If you debit and credit the wrong accounts the trial balance will still balance, even though there is an error.

**Trial Balance of Boyd Ltd as on 1 February**

| | DR | CR |
|---|---|---|
| Bank | 54,700 | |
| Share Capital | | 150,000 |
| Premises | 90,000 | |
| Purchases | 6,600 | |
| Sales | | 4,500 |
| Cash | 2,000 | |
| Wages | 1,000 | |
| Sales Returns | 200 | |
| | 154,500 | 154,500 |

## 2.4 LEDGERS

The place where accounts are stored are called Ledgers. Traditionally a ledger is a book but nowadays many ledgers are kept on computer spreadsheets and are only printed out when necessary. Computerised accounts, while they save time and labour, do not remove the need to understand how to record financial information in an account.

As a business may have hundreds of accounts, the ledgers are usually divided in three sections:

### 1. Debtors Ledger (DL)

This contains all the accounts of the business's debtors (people who owe the business money).

### 2. Creditors Ledger (CL)

This contains all the accounts of the business's creditors (people who the business owes money to).

### 3. General Ledger (GL)

This contains all the other asset, liability, expense and revenue accounts.

*Folios*

Now we use GL, DL and CL together with the page number of the other account involved in a transaction. This tells a bookkeeper not only which page of a ledger an account is on but also which of the three ledgers the account can be found in.

*Example*

The following are the transactions of Laing Ltd for May 2000. Post these transactions to the relevant ledgers, balance the accounts and extract a trial balance on the 1st June 2000.

| | |
|---|---|
| 1 May | Issued 200,000 IR£1 Ordinary shares, money was lodged |
| 2 May | Purchased machinery for IR£20,000 by cheque |
| 5 May | Purchased goods for IR£3,000, paid by cheque |
| 9 May | Sold goods for IR£3,000, money was lodged |
| 11 May | Bought goods on credit from J. Boyd Ltd for IR£3,150 |
| 14 May | Paid insurance by cheque, IR£1,000 |
| 14 May | Returned faulty goods to J. Boyd Ltd valued at IR£250 |
| 15 May | Sold goods on credit to J. Nolan, IR£900 |
| 19 May | J. Nolan paid IR£900, money was lodged |
| 27 May | Paid J. Boyd Ltd IR£2,000 by cheque |

SOLUTION

**The Books of Laing Ltd for May 2000**

**General Ledger**

| DR | | **Bank Account (1)** | | | | | CR |
|---|---|---|---|---|---|---|---|
| 1 May | Share Capital | GL2 | 200,000 | 2 May | Machinery | GL3 | 20,000 |
| 9 May | Sales | GL5 | 3,000 | 5 May | Purchases | GL4 | 3,000 |
| 19 May | J. Nolan | DL1 | 900 | 14 May | Insurance | GL6 | 1,000 |
| | | | | 27 May | J. Boyd Ltd | CL1 | 2,000 |
| | | | | 31 May | Balance c/d | | 177,900 |
| | | | 203,900 | | | | 203,900 |
| 1 Jun | Balance b/d | | 177,900 | | | | |

| DR | | **Share Capital Account (2)** | | | | | CR |
|---|---|---|---|---|---|---|---|
| | | | | 1 May | Bank | GL1 | 200,000 |

| DR | | **Machinery Account (3)** | | | | | CR |
|---|---|---|---|---|---|---|---|
| 2 May | Bank | GL1 | 20,000 | | | | |

| DR | Purchases Account (4) | | | | | | CR |
|---|---|---|---|---|---|---|---|
| 5 May | Bank | GL1 | 3,000 | | | | |
| 11 May | J. Boyd Ltd | CL1 | 3,150 | 31 May | Balance c/d | | 6,150 |
| | | | 6,150 | | | | 6,150 |
| 1 Jun | Balance b/d | | 6,150 | | | | |

| DR | Sales Account (5) | | | | | | CR |
|---|---|---|---|---|---|---|---|
| | | | | 9 May | Bank | GL1 | 3,000 |
| 31 May | Balance c/d | | 3,900 | 19 May | J. Nolan | DL1 | 900 |
| | | | 3,900 | | | | 3,900 |
| | | | | 1 Jun | Balance b/d | | 3,900 |

| DR | Insurance Account (6) | | | | | | CR |
|---|---|---|---|---|---|---|---|
| 14 May | Bank | GL1 | 1,000 | | | | |

| DR | Purchase Returns Account (7) | | | | | | CR |
|---|---|---|---|---|---|---|---|
| | | | | 14 May | J. Boyd | CL1 | 250 |

**Creditors Ledger**

| DR | J. Boyd Ltd (1) | | | | | | CR |
|---|---|---|---|---|---|---|---|
| 14 May | Purchase Rtns | GL7 | 250 | 11 May | Purchases | GL4 | 3,150 |
| 27 May | Bank | GL1 | 2,000 | | | | |
| 31 May | Balance c/d | | 900 | | | | |
| | | | 3,150 | | | | 3,150 |
| | | | | 1 Jun | Balance b/d | | 900 |

**Debtors Ledger**

| DR | J. Nolan Account (1) | | | | | | CR |
|---|---|---|---|---|---|---|---|
| 15 May | Sales | GL5 | 900 | 19 May | Bank | GL1 | 900 |

**Trial Balance of Laing Ltd as on 1 June 2000**

| | DR | CR |
|---|---|---|
| Bank | 177,900 | |
| Share Capital | | 200,000 |
| Machinery | 20,000 | |
| Purchases | 6,150 | |
| Sales | | 3,900 |
| Insurance | 1,000 | |
| Purchase Returns | | 250 |
| Creditor: J. Boyd Ltd | | 900 |
| | 205,050 | 205,050 |

## 2.5 ANALYSED CASH BOOK

Because the Bank and Cash Accounts in the General Ledger contain more transactions than other accounts, they are given their own book, the Cash Book. There are two accepted ways of laying out the Cash Book:

### 1. Two Stand-Alone Analysed Books and a Bank Account

- ► An Analysed Cash Receipts and Lodgements Book
- ► An Analysed Cash and Cheque Payments Book
- ► Coupled with a Bank and Cash Account in the General Ledger

The Analysed Cash Receipts and Lodgement Book and Analysed Cash and Cheque Payments Book only include receipts and payments.

The Bank and Cash Accounts show Opening Balances, Total Receipts (taken from the Analysed Cash Receipts and Lodgement Book), Total Payments (taken from the Analysed Cash and Cheque Payments Book) and finally a Closing Balance (calculated from the above in the usual way).

### 2. An Analysed Cash Book

A coming together of all three elements of the above. The Analysed Cash Book is a normal T-Account (with a debit and credit side), like the Analysed Cash Receipts and Lodgements and Cash and Cheque Payments Books it has extra columns that allow a business to see at a glance how much it has paid for purchases, received for sales etc. It also includes Opening Balances and Closing Balances for the bank column, therefore a separate T-Account in the General Ledger is not necessary.

The total for the analysis columns is then posted to the relevant accounts in the ledgers. Note that only the Bank and Cash columns are balanced.

*Figure 2.3 — Sources for Cash Book, Analysed Cash Receipts, Lodgement Book, Analysed Cash and Cheque Payments Book*

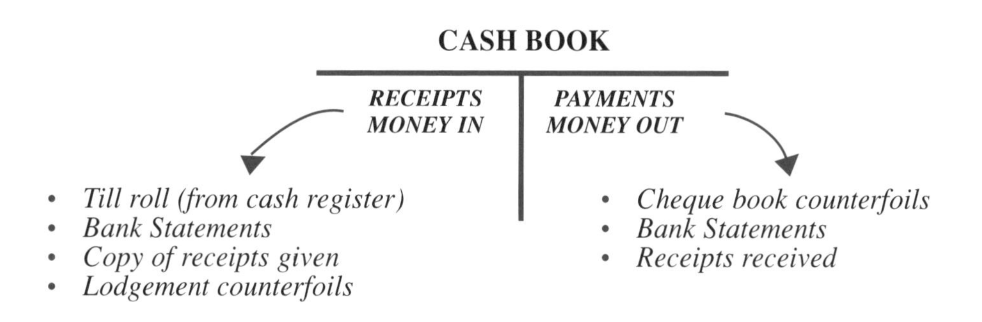

*Example*

Record the following transactions of Hamill Ltd in the Cash Book, using the following headings:

***Debit Side:*** *Debtors, Sales.*
***Credit Side:*** *Wages, Creditors, Purchases.*

| | |
|---|---|
| 1 July | Cash at bank IR£6,500 (Opening Balance) |
| 9 July | Purchases goods by cheque (No. 15), IR£1,550 |
| 11 July | Paid wage by cheque (No. 16), IR£4,000 |
| 14 July | Cash sales, IR£3,950 |
| 14 July | Paid Devlin Ltd by cheque (No. 17), IR£1,300 |
| 15 July | Purchased goods by cash, IR£450 |
| 15 July | Received cheque from Gavin Ltd, IR£1,000 lodged |

SOLUTION — METHOD I

**Analysed Cash Receipts and Lodgements Book of Hamill Ltd**

| Date | Details | Bank | Cash | Debtors | Sales |
|---|---|---|---|---|---|
| 14.7.99 | Sales | | 3,950 | | 3,950 |
| 15.7.99 | Gavin Ltd | 1,000 | | 1,000 | |
| | | 1,000 | 3,950 | 1,000 | 3,950 |

**Analysed Cash and Cheque Payments Book of Hamill Ltd**

| Date | Details | Chq No. | Bank | Cash | Wages | Creditors | Purchases |
|---|---|---|---|---|---|---|---|
| 9.7.99 | Purchases | 15 | 1,550 | | | | 1,550 |
| 11.7.99 | Wages | 16 | 4,000 | | 4,000 | | |
| 14.7.99 | Devlin Ltd | 17 | 1,300 | | | 1,300 | |
| 15.7.99 | Purchases | 18 | | 450 | | | 450 |
| | | | 6,850 | 450 | 4,000 | 1,300 | 1,550 |

**Bank Account**

| Date | Details | F | Total | Date | Details | F | Total |
|---|---|---|---|---|---|---|---|
| 1.7.99 | Balance | b/d | 6,500 | 31.7.99 | Payments | ACCP | 6,850 |
| 31.7.99 | Receipts | ACRL | 1,000 | 31.7.99 | Balance | c/d | 650 |
| | | | 7,500 | | | | 7,500 |
| 1.8.99 | Balance | b/d | 650 | | | | |

**Cash Account**

| Date | Details | F | Total | Date | Details | F | Total |
|---|---|---|---|---|---|---|---|
| 31.7.99 | Receipts | ACRL | 3,950 | 31.7.99 | Payments | ACCP | 450 |
| | | | | 31.7.99 | Balance | c/d | 3,500 |
| | | | 3,950 | | | | 3,950 |
| 1.8.99 | Balance | b/d | 3,500 | | | | |

SOLUTION — METHOD II

**Analysed Cash Book of Hamill Ltd**

| Date | Details | Bank | Cash | Debtors | Sales | Date | Details | Chq No. | Bank | Cash | Wages | Creditors | Purchases |
|---|---|---|---|---|---|---|---|---|---|---|---|---|---|
| 1.7.99 | Bal b/d | 6,500 | | | | 9.7.99 | Purchases | 15 | 1,550 | | | | 1,550 |
| 14.7.99 | Sales | | 3,950 | | 3,950 | 11.7.99 | Wages | 16 | 4,000 | | 4,000 | | |
| 15.7.99 | Gavin Ltd | 1,000 | | 1,000 | | 14.7.99 | Devlin Ltd | 17 | 1,300 | | | 1,300 | |
| | | | | | | 15.7.99 | Purchases | 18 | | 450 | | | 450 |
| | | | | | | 31.7.99 | Bal c/d | | 650 | 3500 | | | |
| | | 7,500 | 3,950 | 1,000 | 3,950 | | | | 7,500 | 3,950 | 4,000 | 1,300 | 1,550 |
| 1.8.99 | Bal b/d | 650 | 3,500 | | | | | | | | | | |

**Note** It is important to remember that only the bank and cash columns are balanced. As before, balances brought down are included in the Trial Balance on which ever side they occur.

The Cash Book only records one part of the double entry, it is also necessary to make corresponding entries in the ledgers. They will be on the opposite side to the Cash Book.

For the purpose of this book, Method II will be used from now on — An Analysed Cash Book.

## 2.6 CONTRA ENTRIES

There is an exception to the above rule that every entry in the Cash Book has a corresponding entry in a ledger — a 'CONTRA ENTRY'. This is a transaction that affects both the debit and credit side of the Cash Book. This entails cash being transferred from the Cash Account to the Bank Account and vice versa.

*WITHDREW CASH FROM THE BANK OR LODGED CASH INTO THE BANK*

The two accounts involved are the Cash Account and the Bank Account, both of which are recorded in the Cash Book. Therefore a Contra Entry does not appear in any ledger.

To show a Contra Entry in the Cash Book, we place the letter 'c' or the symbol '©' in the folio column of the Cash Book.

*Example*
5 Oct Withdrew IR£600 cash from bank account

**Cash Book**

| Date | Details | F | Bank | Cash | Date | Details | F | Bank | Cash |
|---|---|---|---|---|---|---|---|---|---|
| 5 Oct | Bank | © | | 600 | 5 Oct | Cash | © | 600 | |

In this case the Bank Account has paid IR£600 into the Cash Account, therefore the Bank is the giver and Cash is the receiver. Note the folio for this Contra Entry.

**Note** For the purpose of the Junior Certificate we normally only include a Bank column in the Cash Book, however, you must be aware of what a Contra Entry is and how to deal with it.

## 2.7 HOW TO DEAL WITH VAT (VALUE ADDED TAX)

Up to now we have assumed that all money paid to the business or all money paid by the business is revenue. This is not the case, when we buy something, only part of what we pay actually goes to the seller, the balance is a tax, Value Added Tax. Businesses collect this tax for the Revenue Commissioners, it is an Indirect Tax.

*Figure 2.4*

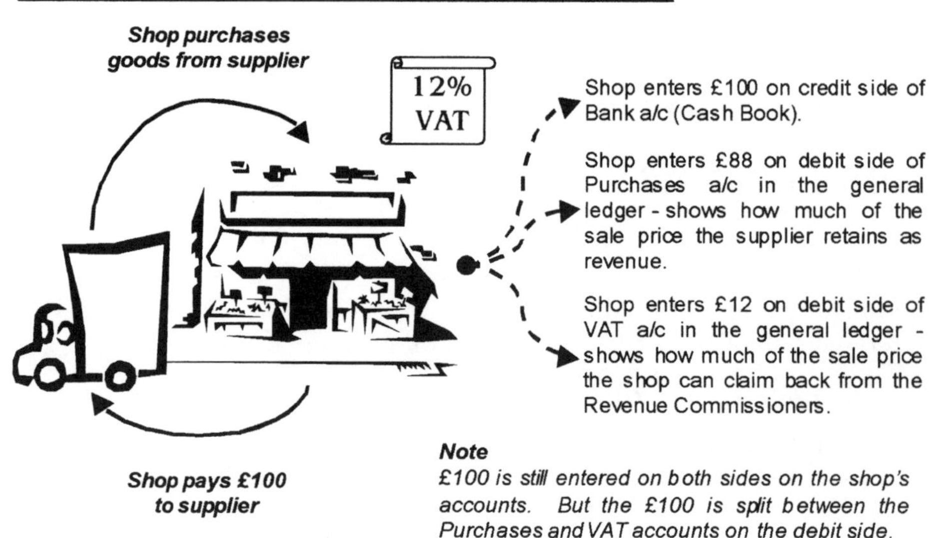

## HOW VAT WORKS: SHOP SELLS GOODS

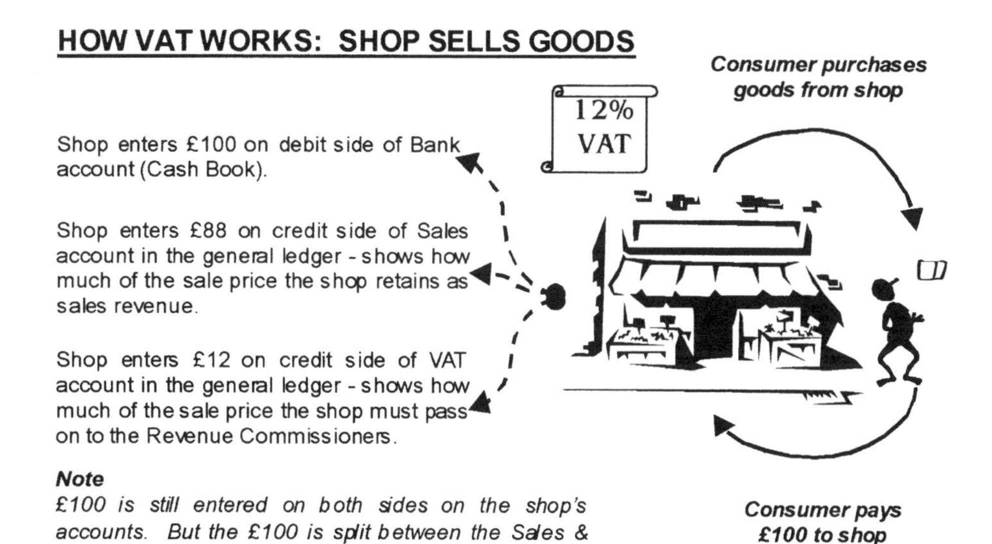


VAT is placed in its own account so that the business has a record of how much it has collected for the Revenue Commissioners. The entry in the VAT account goes on the same side as the related entry (i.e. sales, purchases etc.).

### *Example*

McCann Ltd, a private limited company, was formed on the 1st April, 2000. On that date shareholders invested IR£80,000 and this was lodged to the company bank account.

The following transactions took place during the month of April 2000:

| | | | |
|---|---|---|---|
| 5 Apr | Purchased delivery van | (cheque No. 1) | IR£19,000 |
| 7 Apr | Paid expenses | (cheque No. 2) | IR£3,200 |
| 11 Apr | Cash sales lodged | | IR£14,300 (IR£11,297 + IR£3,003 VAT) |
| 14 Apr | Purchases for resale | (cheque No. 3) | IR£7,500 + VAT 21% |
| 28 Apr | Cash sales lodged | | IR£5,500 (IR£4,345 + IR£1,155 VAT) |
| 29 Apr | Paid Wages | (cheque No. 4) | IR£7,300 |

You are required to:

(a) Enter the transaction of the 1st April, 2000 in the appropriate ledger accounts.

(b) Record the transactions for the month of April in the Cash Book. Post the relevant figures to the ledgers.

**Note** Analyse the bank transactions using the following money column headings:

**Debit (Receipts) Side:** Bank, Sales, VAT, Other.

**Credit (Payments) Side:** Bank, Purchases, VAT, Other.

(c) Balance the accounts on the 30th April, 2000 and extract a Trial Balance as on that date.

*SOLUTION*

## Analysed Cash Book of McCann Ltd

| Date | Details | F | Bank | Sales | VAT | Other | Date | Details | F | Chq No. | Bank | Purchases | VAT | Other |
|---|---|---|---|---|---|---|---|---|---|---|---|---|---|---|
| 1.4.00 | Share Capital | GL1 | 80,000 | | | 80,000 | 5.4.00 | Van | GL2 | 1 | 19,000 | | | 19,000 |
| 11.4.00 | Sales | GL4 | 14,300 | 11,297 | 3,003 | | 5.4.00 | Expenses | GL3 | 2 | 3,200 | | | 3,200 |
| 28.4.00 | Sales | GL4 | 5,500 | 4,345 | 1,155 | | 14.4.00 | Purchases | GL5 | 3 | 9,075 | 7,500 | 1,575 | |
| | | | | | | | 29.4.00 | Wages | GL6 | 4 | 7,300 | | | 7,300 |
| | | | | | | | 30.4.00 | Balance | c/d | | 61,225 | | | |
| | | | 99,800 | 15,642 | 4,158 | 80,000 | | | | | 99,800 | 7,500 | 1,575 | 29,500 |
| 30.4.00 | Balance | b/d | 61,225 | | | | | | | | | | | |

**Ledgers of McCann Ltd for April 1999**

### General Ledger

**Share Capital Account (1)**

| Date | Details | F | Total | Date | Details | F | Total |
|---|---|---|---|---|---|---|---|
| | | | | 1.4.00 | Bank | CB | 80,000 |

**Van Account (2)**

| Date | Details | F | Total | Date | Details | F | Total |
|---|---|---|---|---|---|---|---|
| 5.4.00 | Bank | CB | 19,000 | | | | |

**Expenses Account (3)**

| Date | Details | F | Total | Date | Details | F | Total |
|---|---|---|---|---|---|---|---|
| 7.4.00 | Bank | CB | 3,200 | | | | |

**Sales Account (4)**

| Date | Details | F | Total | Date | Details | F | Total |
|---|---|---|---|---|---|---|---|
| | | | | 11.4.00 | Bank | CB | 11,297 |
| 30.4.00 | Balance | c/d | 15,642 | 28.4.00 | Bank | CB | 4,345 |
| | | | 15,642 | | | | 15,642 |
| | | | | 30.4.00 | Balance | b/d | 15,642 |

**Purchases Account (5)**

| Date | Details | F | Total | Date | Details | F | Total |
|---|---|---|---|---|---|---|---|
| 14.4.00 | Bank | CB | 7,500 | | | | |

**Wages Account (6)**

| | | | | | | | |
|---|---|---|---|---|---|---|---|
| 29.4.00 | Bank | CB | 7,300 | | | | |

**VAT Account (7)**

| | | | | | | | |
|---|---|---|---|---|---|---|---|
| 14.4.00 | Purchases | GL5 | 1,575 | 11.4.00 | Sales | GL4 | 3,003 |
| 30.4.00 | Balance | c/d | 2,583 | 28.4.00 | Sales | GL4 | 1,155 |
| | | | 4,158 | | | | 4,158 |
| | | | | 30.4.00 | Balance | b/d | 2,583 |

**Trial Balance of McCann Ltd as on 30 April 2000**

| | DR | CR |
|---|---|---|
| Bank | 61,225 | |
| Share Capital | | 80,000 |
| Van | 19,000 | |
| Expenses | 3,200 | |
| Sales | | 15,642 |
| Purchases | 7,500 | |
| Wages | 7,300 | |
| VAT | | 2,583 |
| | 98,225 | 98,225 |

**Notes**

- Often in Junior Certificate questions you are given one transaction at the start of the question which can easily be forgotten. In this case it is the issuing of shares to investors on the first of the month.
- The figures entered in the sales and purchases accounts are net of VAT. They can be taken from the sales and purchases columns in the cash book.
- VAT is entered on the same side as the transaction it relates to, i.e. sales or purchases in this case.

## Practice Questions

1. Record the following transactions of Macomber Ltd in the Analysed Cash Book. Post the relevant figures to the ledgers, balance the accounts and extract a Trial Balance as on the last day of the month.

| | | | |
|---|---|---|---|
| 3 Jan | Purchases for resale | (cheque No. 41) | €10,500 + VAT 12% |
| 5 Jan | Paid wages | (cheque No. 42) | €4,000 |

| | | | |
|---|---|---|---|
| 7 Jan | Cash sales lodged | | €7,500 (€6,600 + €900 VAT) |
| 10 Jan | Purchased goods on credit from Sammy Ltd | | €8,000 + VAT 12% |
| 13 Jan | Cash sales lodges | | €14,000 (€12,320 + €1,680 VAT) |
| 15 Jan | Paid ESB | (cheque No. 43) | €350 |

**Note** Analyse the bank transactions using the following column headings:

***Debit Side:*** *Sales, VAT.*
***Credit Side:*** *Purchases, VAT, Other.*

2. Record the following transactions of Barford Ltd in the Analysed Cash Book. Post the relevant figures to the ledgers, balance the accounts and extract a Trial Balance as on the last day of the month.

| | | | |
|---|---|---|---|
| 1 Mar | Cash Sales lodged | | €21,500 (€18,920 + €2,580 VAT) |
| 4 Mar | Purchases for resale | (cheque No. 5) | €14,000 + VAT 12% |
| 7 Mar | Paid rent | (cheque No. 6) | €5,400 |
| 9 Mar | Cash sales lodged | | €53,000 (€46,640 + €6,360 VAT) |
| 18 Mar | Paid wages | (cheque No. 7) | €21,200 |
| 23 Mar | Shareholders invest | | €45,000 |
| 25 Mar | Sold goods on Credit to Adams Ltd | | €13,500 + VAT 12% |
| 29 Mar | Paid insurance | (cheque No. 8) | €9,000 |

**Note** Analyse the bank transactions using the following column headings:

***Debit Side:*** *Sales, VAT, Other.*
***Credit Side:*** *Purchases, VAT, Other.*

3. Record the following transactions of Fred Ltd in the Analysed Cash Book. Post the relevant figures to the ledgers, balance the accounts and extract a Trial Balance as on the last day of the month.

| | | | |
|---|---|---|---|
| 4 Dec | Cash sales lodged | | IR£54,200 (IR£47,696 + IR£6,504 VAT) |
| 5 Dec | Paid advertising | (cheque No. 21) | IR£32,000 |
| 8 Dec | Purchased goods on credit from Lee Ltd | | IR£20,000 + VAT 12% |
| 12 Dec | Sold goods on credit to Suker Ltd | | IR£18,000 (IR£15,840 + IR£2,160 VAT) |
| 14 Dec | Paid insurance | (cheque No. 22) | IR£4,000 |

| | | | |
|---|---|---|---|
| 21 Dec | Suker Ltd paid in full | | |
| 23 Dec | Paid Lee Ltd in full | (cheque No. 23) | |

**Note** Analyse the bank transactions using the following column headings:

***Debit Side:*** *Sales, VAT, Debtors.*
***Credit Side:*** *Creditors, Other.*

4. Record the following transactions of Parke Ltd in the Analysed Cash Book. Post the relevant figures to the ledgers, balance the accounts and extract a Trial Balance as on the last day of the month.

| | | | |
|---|---|---|---|
| 4 Jan | Purchased goods on credit from Dixon Ltd | | €4,700 + VAT 21% |
| 7 Jan | Paid Petty Cash | (cheque No. 40) | €300 |
| 13 Jan | Cash Sales lodged | | €24,000 (€18,960 + €5,040) |
| 15 Jan | Purchased van | (cheque No. 41) | €18,000 + VAT 21% |
| 19 Jan | Paid wages | (cheque No. 42) | €23,000 |
| 20 Jan | Cash sales lodged | | €36,000 (€32,000 + €4,000 VAT) |
| 21 Jan | Paid Dixon Ltd in full | (cheque No. 43) | |

**Note** Analyse the bank transactions using the following column headings:

***Debit Side:*** *Sales, VAT.*
***Credit Side:*** *Purchases, VAT, Creditors, Other.*

## 2.8 PETTY CASH BOOK

Apart from large transactions passing through the Analysed Cash Book, businesses also have many small expenses to meet, such as stamps, tea and coffee for the staff canteen, petrol etc. The Petty Cash Book is used to record these small cash transactions. It is a special analysed cash book with analysis columns.

The Petty Cash Book operates a IMPREST system. An imprest is a float, paid at the start of the month. It is entered on the debit side of the Petty Cash Book.

When employees want to claim an expense they complete a Petty Cash Voucher, with is presented to the person in charge of petty cash. This voucher is the source document for the credit side to the Petty Cash Book.

At the end of a given period (e.g. a week, a month) the Petty Cash Book is balanced and the imprest restored from the Cash Book.

The expense columns are totalled and the totals are posted to the ledger. Posting the total figures saves us posting each entry individually.

A Petty Cash Voucher should include the following information:

- A reference/voucher number
- Date
- Details/reason for claim
- Claimants signature
- Supervisors signature

*Figure 2.5*

**PETTY CASH VOUCHER** **No. 56**

For What Required Date: 1.5.99

Amount: IR£6·00

20 stamps at 30p each

Signature: Ken Barlow

Passed by: Curly Watts

***Example***

Record the following transactions in the Petty Cash Book of Coxy Ltd for July 2001, using the following column headings:

*Postage, Motor, Canteen, Sundries.*

Balance the Petty Cash Book and post the expense to the ledger.

| | |
|---|---|
| 1 July | Cash on hand (imprest), IR£100·00 |
| 9 July | Coffee, IR£5·30, voucher No. 12 |
| 11 July | Petrol, IR£22·50, voucher No. 13 |
| 14 July | Stamps, IR£6·00, voucher No. 14 |
| 14 July | Sugar, IR£1·20, voucher No. 15 |
| 15 July | Motor oil, IR£5·60, voucher No. 16 |
| 16 July | Stamps, IR£12·00, voucher No. 17 |
| 17 July | Paid window cleaner, IR£25·00, voucher No. 18 |
| 18 July | Taxi, IR£15·00, voucher No. 19 |
| 1 August | Received cheque to restore imprest |

## SOLUTION

### *Petty Cash Book of Coxy Ltd*

| Date | Details | F | Cash | Date | Details | Voucher No. | Cash Paid | Postage | Motor | Staff canteen | Sundries |
|---|---|---|---|---|---|---|---|---|---|---|---|
| 1.7.01 | Balance | b/d | 100·00 | 9.7.01 | Coffee | 12 | 5·30 | | | 5·30 | |
| | | | | 11.7.01 | Petrol | 13 | 22·50 | | 22·50 | | |
| | | | | 14.7.01 | Stamps | 14 | 6·00 | 6·00 | | | |
| | | | | 14.7.01 | Sugar | 15 | 1·20 | | | 1·20 | |
| | | | | 15.7.01 | Motor oil | 16 | 5·60 | | 5·60 | | |
| | | | | 16.7.01 | Stamps | 17 | 12·00 | 12·00 | | | |
| | | | | 17.7.01 | Window cleaner | 18 | 25·00 | | | | 25·00 |
| | | | | 18.7.01 | Taxi | 19 | 15·00 | | | | 15·00 |
| | | | | 31.7.01 | Balance | c/d | 7·40 | | | | |
| | | | 100·00 | | | | 100·00 | 18·00 | 28·10 | 6·50 | 40·00 |
| 1.8.01 | Balance | b/d | 7·40 | | | | | | | | |
| 1.8.01 | Bank | CB | 92·60 | | | | | | | | |

### *General Ledger*

**Postage Expenses Account (1)**

| Date | Details | F | Total | Date | Details | F | Total |
|---|---|---|---|---|---|---|---|
| 31.7.01 | Petty cash | PCB | 18·00 | | | | |

**Motor Expense Account (2)**

| Date | Details | F | Total | Date | Details | F | Total |
|---|---|---|---|---|---|---|---|
| 31.7.01 | Petty cash | PCB | 28·10 | | | | |

**Canteen Expenses Account (3)**

| Date | Details | F | Total | Date | Details | F | Total |
|---|---|---|---|---|---|---|---|
| 31.7.01 | Petty cash | PCB | 6·50 | | | | |

**Sundry Expenses Account (4)**

| Date | Details | F | Total | Date | Details | F | Total |
|---|---|---|---|---|---|---|---|
| 31.7.01 | Petty cash | PCB | 40·00 | | | | |

## Practice Questions

1. Record the following transactions in the Petty Cash Book of Office Supplies Ltd for December 2005, using the following column headings:

   *Stationery, Motor, Canteen, Sundries.*

   Balance the Petty Cash Book and post the expense to the ledger.

| | |
|---|---|
| 1 December | Cash on hand (imprest), €150·00 |
| 3 December | Envelopes, €8·50, voucher No. 46 |
| 5 December | Petrol, €27·00, voucher No. 47 |
| 6 December | Washing up liquid, €1·25, voucher No. 48 |
| 8 December | Paper, €5·99, voucher No. 49 |
| 12 December | Folders, €12·00, voucher No. 50 |
| 14 December | Decorations, €25·00, voucher No. 51 |
| 20 December | Taxi, €35·00, voucher No. 52 |
| 21 December | New kettle, €14·00, voucher No. 53 |
| 1 January | Received cheque to restore imprest |

2. Record the following transactions in the Petty Cash Book of Lovejoy Ltd for April 2003, using the following column headings:

   *Motor, Travel, Sundries.*

   Balance the Petty Cash Book and post the expense to the ledger.

| | |
|---|---|
| 1 April | Cash on hand (imprest), €90·00 |
| 4 April | Petrol, €20·00, voucher No. 127 |
| 7 April | Train fare, €5·00, voucher No. 128 |
| 10 April | Cleaner's pay, €20·00, voucher No. 129 |
| 13 April | Bus fare, €1·20, voucher No. 130 |
| 17 April | Motor oil, €5.00, voucher No. 131 |
| 21 April | Petrol, €10·00, voucher No. 132 |
| 27 April | Taxi, €10·00, voucher No. 133 |
| 1 May | Received cheque to restore imprest |

3. Record the following transactions in the Petty Cash Book of Clancy Ltd for June 2004, using the following column headings:

   *Cleaning, Travel, Stationery, Sundries.*

   Balance the Petty Cash Book and post the expense to the ledger.

| | |
|---|---|
| 1 June | Cash on hand (imprest), €200·00 |
| 2 June | Paid window cleaner, €20·00, voucher No. 9 |
| 5 June | Business cards, €15·00, voucher No. 10 |
| 7 June | Train fare, €23·00, voucher No. 11 |
| 9 June | Paid cleaner, €10·00, voucher No. 12 |

| | |
|---|---|
| 14 June | Paper, €6·00, voucher No. 13 |
| 16 June | New toaster, €14·00, voucher No. 14 |
| 23 June | Taxi, €9·00, voucher No. 15 |
| 1 July | Received cheque to restore imprest |

4. Record the following transactions in the Petty Cash Book of Francis Ltd for August 2006, using the following column headings:

   *Postage, Motor, Travel, Sundries.*

   Balance the Petty Cash Book and post the expense to the ledger.

| | |
|---|---|
| 1 August | Cash on hand (imprest), €100·00 |
| 4 August | Stamps, €6·00, voucher No. 31 |
| 7 August | Petrol, €22·00, voucher No. 32 |
| 8 August | Taxi, €8·50, voucher No. 33 |
| 13 August | Stamps, €0·90, voucher No. 34 |
| 17 August | Car wash, €4·50, voucher No. 35 |
| 21 August | Train fare, €32·00, voucher No. 36 |
| 27 August | Donation, €4·00, voucher No. 37 |
| 1 September | Received cheque to restore imprest |

## 2.9 DAY BOOKS

In the real world many business transactions are on 'CREDIT', in other words customers do not pay for the goods at the time of purchase but at a later date. This is particularly common with intra-business trade.

It is important that a business keeps a record of all credit transactions so that it knows how much it is due and it owed in terms of credit sales and purchases. The Cash Book and Ledgers do not really provide a suitable place to register these transactions, so we open DAY BOOKS.

There are four Day Books:

***Purchases Day Book (PDB)***

- Records goods purchased by the business on credit

***Purchase Returns Day Book (PRDB)***

- Records returns of goods purchased on credit

***Sales Day Book (SDB)***

- Records goods sold by the business on credit

***Sales Returns Day Book (SRDB)***

- Records returns of goods sold on credit by the business

## Sources

There are two documents we should be concerned with for the Day Books.

*Invoice*

This is the business equivalent of a bill, like your telephone or ESB bill at home. It details goods purchased without prior payment. At home you utilise electricity and use your phone normally for a two month period before payment is requested. Essentially the same happens in business. When you purchase/sell goods, you receive/send an invoice detailing seller's and buyer's name; an invoice reference number; the date; the amount before VAT (net); the VAT amount and the total (net + VAT).

Invoices are received by a business when it buys on credit and invoices are sent by a business when it sells on credit.

*Credit Note*

This is used when goods received are faulty or damaged. These goods are returned to the seller, who then issues a credit note for the value of the damaged goods. When damaged goods are returned by you or to you, a credit note is issued detailing seller's and buyer's name; a credit note reference number; the date; the amount before VAT (net); the VAT amount and the total including VAT.

- Seller writes up the SDB from invoices sent.
- Purchaser writes up the PDB from invoices received.
- Seller writes up the SRDB from credit notes sent.
- Purchaser writes up the PRDB from credit notes received.

## Format of Day Books

| Sales and Purchases Day Books | | | | | | |
|---|---|---|---|---|---|---|
| Date | Details | Invoice No. | Folio | Net | VAT | Total |
| | | | | | | |

| Sales Returns and Purchase Returns Day Books | | | | | | |
|---|---|---|---|---|---|---|
| Date | Details | Credit Note No. | Folio | Net | VAT | Total |
| | | | | | | |

## Posting the Day Books

*Figure 2.6*

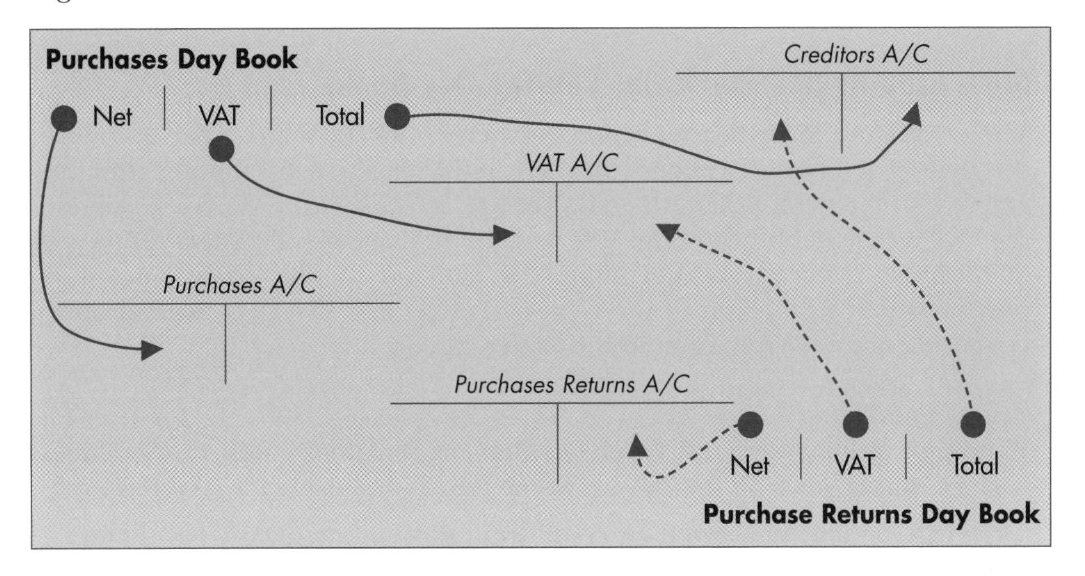


*Figure 2.7*

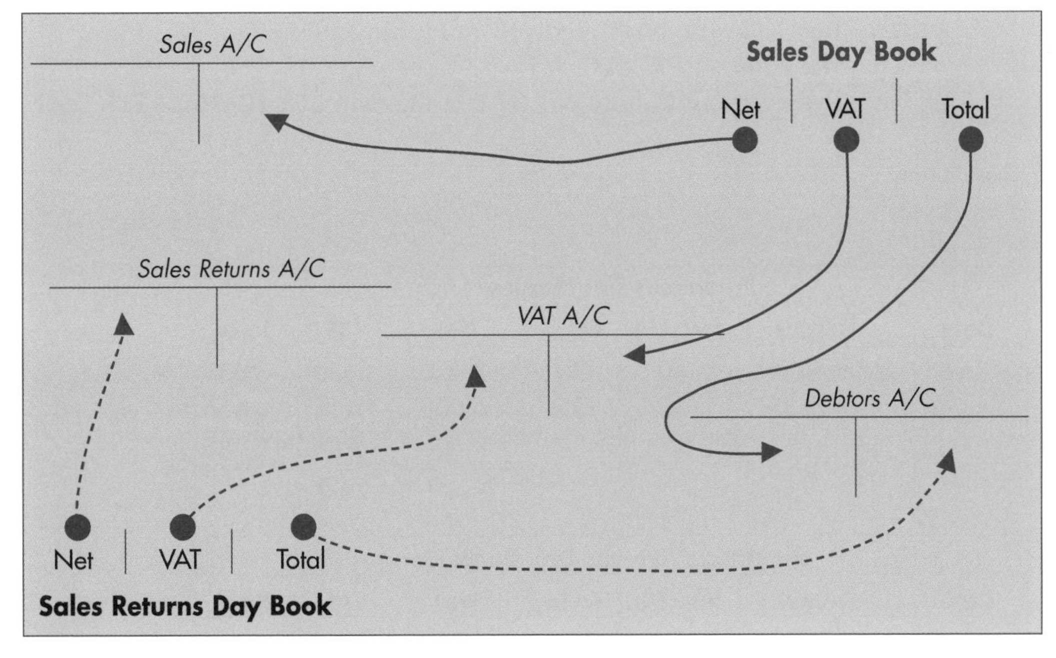


## Sales and Purchases Day Books

The total figure for each transaction is entered into the appropriate account in the Debtor or Creditor Ledgers. In the case of sales, the net amount is entered on the credit side of the sales account in the general ledger and the VAT on the credit side of the VAT account in the General Ledger. In the case of purchases, the net amount is entered on the debit side of the purchases account in the General Ledger and the VAT element on the debit side of the VAT account in the General Ledger.

## Sales Returns and Purchases Returns Day Books

The total figure for each transaction is entered into the appropriate account in the Debtor or Creditor Ledgers. In the case of sales returns, the net amount is entered on the debit side of the sales returns account in the general ledger and the VAT on the debit side of the VAT account in the General Ledger. In the case of purchases returns, the net amount is entered on the credit side of the purchases returns account in the General Ledger and the VAT element on the credit side of the VAT account in the General Ledger.

**SAMPLE QUESTION**

Write up the Purchases and Purchases Returns Day Books, post to the ledgers, balance the accounts on the last day of the month and extract a Trial Balance.

- 1 Dec Purchase goods on credit from Killeen Ltd, invoice No. 40 for IR£3,000 + 21% VAT
- 12 Dec Returned goods to Killeen Ltd, received credit note No. 21, IR£500 + 21% VAT
- 14 Dec Purchase goods on credit from Frewin Ltd, invoice No. 13 for IR£5,500 + 21% VAT
- 28 Dec Received credit note No. 27 from Frewin Ltd, IR£100 + 21% VAT

**SOLUTION**

***Day Books***

| Purchases Day Book (1) | | | | | | |
|---|---|---|---|---|---|---|
| **Date** | **Details** | **Inv. No.** | **Folio** | **Net** | **VAT** | **Total** |
| 1 Dec | Killeen Ltd | 40 | CL1 | 3,000 | 630 | 3,630 |
| 14 Dec | Frewin Ltd | 13 | CL2 | 5,500 | 1,155 | 6,655 |
| | | | | 8,500 | 1,785 | 10,285 |
| | | | | *(GL1)* | *(GL2)* | |

| Purchases Returns Day Book (1) | | | | | | |
|---|---|---|---|---|---|---|
| **Date** | **Details** | **Inv. No.** | **Folio** | **Net** | **VAT** | **Total** |
| 12 Dec | Killeen Ltd | 21 | CL1 | 500 | 105 | 605 |
| 28 Dec | Frewin | 27 | CL2 | 100 | 21 | 121 |
| | | | | 600 | 126 | 726 |
| | | | | *(GL3)* | *(GL2)* | |

## *General Ledger*

| DR | | Purchases Account (1) | | | | | CR |
|---|---|---|---|---|---|---|---|
| 14 Dec | Net credit purchases | PDB1 | 8,500 | | | | |

| DR | | VAT Account (2) | | | | | CR |
|---|---|---|---|---|---|---|---|
| 14 Dec | Credit purchases | PDB1 | 1,785 | 28 Dec | Purchase Returns | PDB1 | 126 |
| | | | | 31 Dec | Balance c/d | | 1,659 |
| | | | 1,785 | | | | 1,785 |
| 1 Jan | Balance b/d | | 1,659 | | | | |

| DR | | Purchase Returns Account (3) | | | | | CR |
|---|---|---|---|---|---|---|---|
| | | | | 28 Dec | Credit purchase returns | PRDB1 | 600 |

## *Creditors Ledger*

| DR | | Killeen Ltd Account (1) | | | | | CR |
|---|---|---|---|---|---|---|---|
| 12 Dec | Purchase returns | PRDB1 | 605 | 1 Dec | Credit purchases | PDB1 | 3,630 |
| 31 Dec | Balance c/d | | 3,025 | | | | |
| | | | 3,630 | | | | 3,630 |
| | | | | 1 Jan | Balance b/d | | 3,025 |

| DR | | Frewin Ltd Account (2) | | | | | CR |
|---|---|---|---|---|---|---|---|
| 28 Dec | Purchase returns | PRDB1 | 121 | 14 Dec | Credit purchases | PDB1 | 6,655 |
| 31 Dec | Balance c/d | | 6,534 | | | | |
| | | | 6,655 | | | | 6,655 |
| | | | | 1 Jan | Balance b/d | | 6,534 |

*Trial Balance as on 1 January*

| | DR | CR |
|---|---|---|
| Purchases | 8,500 | |
| VAT | 1,659 | |
| Purchase Returns | | 600 |
| Creditor — Killeen Ltd | | 3,025 |
| Creditor — Frewin Ltd | | 6,534 |
| | 10,159 | 10,159 |

## Practice Questions

For the following questions write up the Day Books, post to the ledgers, balance the accounts on the last day of the month and extract a Trial Balance.

1. 12.01.01 Purchased goods on credit from Parlour Ltd, invoice No. 40, IR£13,000 + 12½% VAT.
   14.01.01 Purchased goods on credit from Wreh Ltd, invoice No. 12, IR£16,000 + 12½% VAT.
   21.01.01 Returned goods to Parlour Ltd, credit note No. 13, IR£800 + 12½% VAT.

2. 09.03.06 Sold goods on credit to Overmars Ltd, invoice No. 13, €42,000 + 21% VAT.
   19.03.06 Sold goods on credit to Seaman Ltd, invoice No. 14, €9,000 + 21% VAT.
   23.03.06 Overmars Ltd returned goods, credit note No. 8, €1,200 + 21% VAT.

3. 02.06.05 Sold goods on credit to Wenger Ltd, invoice No. 14, €17,000 + 12% VAT.
   05.06.05 Purchased goods on credit from Rice Ltd, invoice No. 51, €43,500 + 12% VAT.
   13.06.05 Sold goods on credit to Manninger Ltd, invoice No. 15, €9,800 + 12% VAT.

4. 01.03.07 Sold goods on credit to Keown Ltd, invoice No. 13, €47,000 + 12% VAT.
   08.03.07 Purchased goods on credit from Bergkamp Ltd, invoice No. 73, €53,500 + 12% VAT.
   13.03.07 Sold goods on credit to Ljungberg Ltd, invoice No. 14, €24,800 + 12% VAT.

17.03.07 Keown Ltd returned goods, credit note No. 13, €2,000 + 12% VAT.

## 2.10 GENERAL JOURNAL

The General Journal is used to record those transactions that are not recorded elsewhere in the books of first entry. The following are included in the General Journal: opening balances of assets and liabilities; purchases and sales of fixed assets on credit and written off debts.

The layout of the General Journal is similar to that a trial balance.

*Figure 2.8 — Layout of General Journal*

| Date | Details | Folio | Debit | Credit |
|---|---|---|---|---|
| | *Account names* | A/C folio in ledgers | Assets | Liabilities |
| | *Narration* | | | |

### Dealing with Opening Balances

- All assets are entered into the Debit column
- All liabilities are entered into the Credit column

The difference between asset and liabilities balances is called Share Capital, it is always entered in the credit column.

At the end of the General Journal you must enter a narration. It is a brief description of the transactions in the journal.

*Posting from the General Journal to the Ledgers*

All entries in the debit column of the General Journal are posted to their relevant accounts in the ledgers as balances on the debit side.

All entries in the credit column of the General Journal are posted to their relevant accounts in the ledgers as balances on the credit side.

**Sample Question**

The following are the assets and liabilities of Hollwey Ltd on 1 June. Enter these balances in the General Journal and post to the ledger.

Buildings IR£90,000
Creditor — Klinkenberg Ltd IR£30,000
Bank loan IR£18,000
Debtor — Capel Ltd IR£4,200

*The first step is to distinguish between assets and liabilities, all assets are entered in the debit column, all liabilities are entered in the credit columns.*

*The second step is to calculate Share Capital (Share Capital = Assets – Liabilities).*

### *General Journal*

| Date | Details | Folio | Debit | Credit |
|---|---|---|---|---|
| 1 June | *Assets* | | | |
| | Buildings | GL1 | 90,000 | |
| | Debtor — Capel Ltd | DL1 | 4,200 | |
| | *Liabilities* | | | |
| | Creditor — Klinkenberg Ltd | CL1 | | 30,000 |
| | Bank loan | CB1 | | 18,000 |
| | Share Capital | GL2 | | 46,200 |
| | | | 94,200 | 94,200 |
| | *Assets, liabilities and Share Capital of Hollwey Ltd on 1 June* | | | |

### *General Ledger*

| DR | | Building Account (1) | | | | | CR |
|---|---|---|---|---|---|---|---|
| 1 June | Balance | GJ1 | 90,000 | | | | |

| DR | | Share Capital Account (2) | | | | | CR |
|---|---|---|---|---|---|---|---|
| | | | | 1 June | Balance | GJ1 | 46,200 |

### *Creditors Ledger*

| DR | | Klinkenberg Ltd Account (1) | | | | | CR |
|---|---|---|---|---|---|---|---|
| | | | | 1 June | Balance | GJ1 | 30,000 |

*Debtors Ledger*

| DR | | Capel Ltd Account (1) | | | | | CR |
|---|---|---|---|---|---|---|---|
| 1 June | Balance | GJ1 | 4,200 | | | | |

*Cash Book*

| DR | | Cash Book | | | | | CR |
|---|---|---|---|---|---|---|---|
| | | | | 1 June | Balance | GJ1 | 18,000 |

## 1999 Junior Certificate Question and Solution

**1. Answer ALL SECTIONS. This is a Book of First Entry and Ledger questions.**

The books of FERGO Ltd showed the following balances on 1st May, 1999:

| | IR£ |
|---|---|
| Machinery | 80,000 |
| Creditor: Irwin Ltd | 22,000 |

(A) Enter these balances in the GENERAL JOURNAL, find the ORDINARY SHARE CAPITAL balance and post these balances to the ledgers. (8)

(B) Post the relevant figures from the Sales Book and Purchases Book below to the ledgers. (8)

**SALES DAY BOOK** (Page 1)

| Date | Details | Invoice No. | Folio | Net | VAT | Total |
|---|---|---|---|---|---|---|
| 4.5.99 | Keane Ltd | 17 | DL5 | £56,000 | £7,000 | £63,000 |

**PURCHASES DAY BOOK** (Page 2)

| Date | Details | Invoice No. | Folio | Net | VAT | Total |
|---|---|---|---|---|---|---|
| 9.5.99 | Irwin Ltd | 34 | CL9 | £24,000 | £3,000 | £27,000 |

(C) Record the following Bank Transactions for the month of May. Post relevant figures to the ledger.

**Note** Analyse the transactions using the following money column headings:

**Debit (Receipts) side:** Bank, Sales, VAT, Debtors.

**Credit (Payments) side:** Bank, Purchases, VAT, Creditors, Insurance.

**BANK TRANSACTIONS**

| | | | |
|---|---|---|---|
| 4.5.99 | Paid Insurance | (cheque No. 1) | IR£3,500 |
| 7.5.99 | Cash Sales lodged | | IR£36,000 (IR£32,000 + IR£4,000) |
| 13.5.99 | Paid Irwin Ltd | (cheque No. 2) | IR£40,000 |
| 21.5.99 | Purchases for resale | (cheque No. 3) | IR£20,000 + VAT 12½% |
| 28.5.99 | Keane Ltd paid its account in full which was lodged (receipt No. 78) | | |

(17)

(D) Balance the accounts on the 31st May, 1999 and extract a Trial Balance as on that date. (7)

(40 marks)

**SOLUTION**

ACCOUNTS OF FERGO LTD MAY 1999

*General Journal*

| Date | Details | Folio | Debit | Credit |
|---|---|---|---|---|
| 1.5.99 | *Assets* | | | |
| | Machinery | GL1 | 80,000 | |
| | *Liabilities* | | | |
| | Creditor — Irwin Ltd | CL9 | | 22,000 |
| | Share Capital | GL2 | | 58,000 |
| | | | 80,000 | 80,000 |
| | *Assets, liabilities and Share Capital of Fergo Ltd on 1 May 1999* | | | |

*General Ledger*

| DR | | | **Machinery Account (1)** | | | | CR |
|---|---|---|---|---|---|---|---|
| 1.5.99 | Balance b/d | GJ | 80,000 | | | | |

| DR | | | **Share Capital Account (2)** | | | | CR |
|---|---|---|---|---|---|---|---|
| | | | | 1.5.99 | Balance b/d | GJ | |
| 58,000 | | | | | | | |

| DR | | Sales Account (3) | | | | | CR |
|---|---|---|---|---|---|---|---|
| | | | | 4.5.99 | Credit sales | SDB | 56,000 |
| 31.5.99 | Balance | c/d | 88,000 | 7.5.99 | Bank | CB | 32,000 |
| | | | 88,000 | | | | 88,000 |
| | | | | 31.5.99 | Balance | b/d | 88,000 |

| DR | | Purchases Account (4) | | | | | CR |
|---|---|---|---|---|---|---|---|
| 9.5.99 | Credit purchases | PDB | 24,000 | | | | |
| 21.5.99 | Bank | CB | 20,000 | 31.5.99 | Balance | c/d | 44,000 |
| | | | 44,000 | | | | 44,000 |
| 31.5.99 | Balance | b/d | 44,000 | | | | |

| DR | | VAT Account (5) | | | | | CR |
|---|---|---|---|---|---|---|---|
| 9.5.99 | Credit purchases | PDB | 3,000 | 4.5.99 | Credit sales | SDB | 7,000 |
| 21.5.99 | Bank | CB | 2,500 | 7.5.99 | Bank | CB | 4,000 |
| 31.5.99 | Balance | c/d | 5,500 | | | | |
| | | | 11,000 | | | | 11,000 |
| | | | | 31.5.99 | Balance | b/d | 5,500 |

| DR | | Insurance Account (6) | | | | | CR |
|---|---|---|---|---|---|---|---|
| 4.5.99 | Bank | CB | 3,500 | | | | |

*Creditors Ledger*

| DR | | Irwin Ltd Account (9) | | | | | CR |
|---|---|---|---|---|---|---|---|
| 13.5.99 | Bank | CB | 40,000 | 1.5.99 | Balance b/d | GJ | 22,000 |
| 31.5.99 | Balance | c/d | 9,000 | 9.5.99 | Credit purchases | PDB | 27,000 |
| | | | 49,000 | | | | 49,000 |
| | | | | 31.5.99 | Balance | b/d | 9,000 |

### *Debtors Ledger*

| DR | | Keane Ltd Account (5) | | | | | CR |
|---|---|---|---|---|---|---|---|
| 4.5.99 | Credit sales | SDB | 63,000 | 28.5.99 | Bank | CB | 63,000 |

### *Cash Book*

DR

| Date | Details | Receipt No. | Folio | Bank | Sales | VAT | Debtors |
|---|---|---|---|---|---|---|---|
| 7.5.99 | Sales | | GL3 | 36,000 | 32,000 | 4,000 | |
| 28.5.99 | Keane Ltd | 78 | DL5 | 63,000 | | | 63,000 |
| | | | | 99,000 | 32,000 | 4,000 | 63,000 |
| 31.5.99 | Balance | | b/d | 33,000 | | | |

CR

| Date | Details | Cheque No. | Folio | Bank | Purchases | VAT | Creditors | Insurance |
|---|---|---|---|---|---|---|---|---|
| 4.5.99 | Insurance | 1 | GL6 | 3,500 | | | | 3,500 |
| 13.5.99 | Irwin Ltd | 2 | CL9 | 40,000 | | | 40,000 | |
| 21.5.99 | Purchases | 3 | GL4 | 22,500 | 20,000 | 2,500 | | |
| 31.5.99 | Balance | | c/d | 33,000 | | | | |
| | | | | 99,000 | 20,000 | 2,500 | 40,000 | 3,500 |

### *Trial Balance as on 31st May 1999*

| Date | Details | Folio | DR | CR |
|---|---|---|---|---|
| | Machinery | GL1 | 80,000 | |
| | Share Capital | GL2 | | 58,000 |
| | Sales | GL3 | | 88,000 |
| | Purchases | GL4 | 44,000 | |
| | VAT | GL5 | | 5,500 |
| | Insurance | GL6 | 3,500 | |
| | Bank | CB | 33,000 | |
| | Creditor — Irwin Ltd | CL9 | | 9,000 |
| | | | 160,500 | 160,500 |

## 2.11 COMBINATION QUESTIONS

1. Arsenal Ltd, is a private limited company. The following transactions took place during the month of December 2000.

**CREDIT TRANSACTIONS**

| | | | |
|---|---|---|---|
| 3.12.00 | Sold goods on credit to Overmars Ltd | Invoice No. 47 | IR£28,000 +12½% VAT |
| 5.12.00 | Sold goods on credit to Petit Ltd | Invoice No. 48 | IR£37,000 + 12½% VAT |
| 18.12.00 | Overmars Ltd returned goods | Credit note No. 13 | IR£6,000 + 12½% VAT |

**BANK TRANSACTIONS**

| | | | |
|---|---|---|---|
| 7.12.00 | Purchased goods for resale | Cheque No. 47 | IR£39,000 + 12½% VAT |
| 14.12.00 | Cash sales lodged | | IR£63,000 (IR£57,000 + IR£6,000 VAT) |
| 19.12.00 | Paid for advertising | Cheque No. 48 | IR£41,000 |
| 22.12.00 | Overmars Ltd paid its account in full | Receipt No. 71 | |
| 23.12.00 | Cash sales lodged | | IR£14,000 (IR£11,750 + IR£2,250 VAT) |

You are required to:

(A) Record the transactions for the month of December in the appropriate books of first entry. Post relevant figures to the ledger.

**Note** Analyse the transactions using the following money column headings:

**Debit (Receipts) side:** Bank, Sales, VAT, Debtors.

**Credit (Payments) side:** Bank, Purchases, VAT, Other.

(B) Balance the accounts on the 31st December 2000 and extract a Trial Balance as on that date.

2. Munday Ltd, is a private limited company. The following transactions took place during the month of January 2004.

**CREDIT TRANSACTIONS**

| | | | |
|---|---|---|---|
| 2.1.04 | Sold goods on credit to Monty Ltd | Invoice No. 7 | €37,000 + 12½% VAT |
| 7.1.04 | Sold goods on credit to Petty Ltd | Invoice No. 8 | €19,000 + 12½% VAT |
| 8.1.04 | Monty Ltd returned goods | Credit note No. 3 | €4,200 + 12½% VAT |

**BANK TRANSACTIONS**

| | | | |
|---|---|---|---|
| 3.1.04 | Shareholders invest, money lodged | | €55,000 |
| 14.1.04 | Purchases for resale | Cheque No. 43 | €18,000 + 12½% VAT |
| 17.1.04 | Paid wages | Cheque No. 44 | €24,000 |
| 19.1.04 | Monty Ltd paid account in full | Receipt No. 14 | |
| 24.1.04 | Paid insurance | Cheque No. 45 | €12,000 |
| 27.1.04 | Cash sales lodged | | €36,000 (€30,000 + €6,000 VAT) |

You are required to:

(A) Record the transactions for the month of January in the appropriate books of first entry. Post relevant figures to the ledger.

**Note** Analyse the transactions using the following money column headings:

**Debit (Receipts) side:** Bank, Sales, VAT, Debtors, Other.

**Credit (Payments) side:** Bank, Purchases, VAT, Other.

(B) Balance the accounts on the 31st January, 2004 and extract a Trial Balance as on that date.

3. The books of Gavin Ltd showed the following balances on 1st June, 2006:

| | € |
|---|---|
| Bank | 120,000 |
| Debtor — O'Leary Ltd | 40,000 |
| Creditor — Ward Ltd | 60,000 |

(A) Enter these balances in the GENERAL JOURNAL, find the ORDINARY SHARE CAPITAL balance and post these balances to the ledgers.

The following transactions took place during the month of June 2006.

**CREDIT TRANSACTIONS**

| | | | |
|---|---|---|---|
| 3.6.06 | Sold goods on credit to O'Leary Ltd | Invoice No. 16 | €15,000 + 12½% VAT |
| 7.6.06 | Purchased goods on credit from Ward Ltd | Invoice No. 48 | €30,000 + 12½% VAT |
| 9.6.06 | Purchased goods on credit from Zef Ltd | Invoice No. 21 | €20,000 + 12½% VAT |

**BANK TRANSACTIONS**

| | | | | |
|---|---|---|---|---|
| 2.6.06 | Cash Sales lodged | | €28,000 | (€22,500 + €5,500 VAT) |
| 9.6.06 | Paid for advertising | Cheque No. 208 | €13,000 | |
| 13.6.06 | Paid Ward Ltd in full | Cheque No. 209 | | |
| 15.6.06 | O'Leary Ltd paid its account in full | Receipt No. 51 | | |
| 23.6.06 | Paid wages | Cheque No. 210 | €23,000 | |

You are required to:

(B) Record the transactions for the month of June in the appropriate books of first entry. Post relevant figures to the ledger.

**Note** Analyse the transactions using the following money column headings:

**Debit (Receipts) side:** Bank, Sales, VAT, Debtors.

**Credit (Payments) side:** Bank, Creditors, Advertising, Wages.

(C) Balance the accounts on the 30th June, 2006 and extract a Trial Balance as on that date.

4. The books of Hynes Ltd showed the following balances on 1st March, 2005:

| | € |
|---|---|
| Machinery | 100,000 |
| Equipment | 70,000 |
| Creditor — Seaman Ltd | 30,000 |

(A) Enter these balances in the GENERAL JOURNAL, find the ORDINARY SHARE CAPITAL balance and post these balances to the ledgers.

(B) Post the relevant figures from the Sales Book and Purchases Book below to the ledgers.

***Sales Book and Purchases Book figures to be posted***

**SALES DAY BOOK**

| Date | Details | Invoice No. | Folio | Net | VAT | Total |
|---|---|---|---|---|---|---|
| 4.3.05 | Murphy Ltd | 18 | DL1 | 47,000 | 5,000 | 52,000 |
| 7.3.05 | D'Arcy Ltd | 19 | DL2 | 19,000 | 2,500 | 21,500 |
| | | | | 66,000 | 7,500 | 73,500 |

**SALES RETURNS DAY BOOK**

| Date | Details | Credit Note No. | Folio | Net | VAT | Total |
|---|---|---|---|---|---|---|
| 12.3.05 | Murphy Ltd | 3 | DL1 | 7,000 | 1,750 | 8,750 |

(C) Record the following Bank Transactions for the month of March. Post relevant figures to the ledger.

**Note** Analyse the transactions using the following money column headings:

**Debit (Receipts) side:** Bank, Sales, VAT, Debtors.

**Credit (Payments) side:** Bank, Purchases, VAT, Creditors, Other.

**BANK TRANSACTIONS**

| | | | |
|---|---|---|---|
| 4.3.05 | Cash sales lodged | | €49,000 (€43,750 + €5,250 VAT) |
| 10.3.05 | Paid rent | Cheque No. 11 | €13,800 |
| 19.3.05 | Purchases for resale | Cheque No. 12 | €18,000 + 12½% VAT |
| 21.3.05 | Murphy Ltd paid its account in full | Receipt No. 13 | |
| 29.3.05 | Paid wages | Cheque No. 13 | €18,500 |
| 30.3.05 | Paid Seaman Ltd in full | Cheque No. 14 | |

(D) Balance the accounts on the 31st March, 2005 and extract a Trial Balance as on that date.

5. The books of Hollie Ltd showed the following balances on 1st June, 2006:

| | € |
|---|---|
| Equipment | 120,000 |
| Debtors — Holst Ltd | 80,000 |
| Bank | 60,000 |
| Creditor — Emma Ltd | 60,000 |

(A) Enter these balances in the GENERAL JOURNAL, find the ORDINARY SHARE CAPITAL balance and post these balances to the ledgers.

The following transactions took place during the month of June 2006.

**CREDIT TRANSACTIONS**

| | | | |
|---|---|---|---|
| 2.6.06 | Purchased goods on credit from Rossco Ltd | Invoice No. 16 | €34,000 + 12½% VAT |
| 7.6.06 | Returned goods to Rossco Ltd | Credit note No. 9 | €3,000 + 12½% VAT |
| 10.6.06 | Purchased goods on credit from Emma Ltd | Invoice No. 13 | €43,000 + 12½% VAT |

**BANK TRANSACTIONS**

| | | | |
|---|---|---|---|
| 4.6.06 | Paid for advertising | Cheque No. 14 | €7,500 |
| 17.6.06 | Cash sales lodged | | €81,000 (€68,000 + €13,000 VAT) |

| | | | |
|---|---|---|---|
| 21.6.06 | Paid Rossco Ltd in full | Cheque No. 15 | |
| 26.6.06 | Bank interest lodged | | €700 |
| 29.6.06 | Cash sales lodged | | €53,000 (€49,000 + €4,000 VAT) |
| 30.6.06 | Holst Ltd paid its account in full | Receipt No. 12 | |

You are required to:

(B) Record the transactions for the month of June in the appropriate books of first entry. Post relevant figures to the ledger.

**Note** Analyse the transactions using the following money column headings:

**Debit (Receipts) side:** Bank, Sales, VAT, Debtors, Other.

**Credit (Payments) side:** Bank, Creditors, Other.

(C) Balance the accounts on the 30th June, 2006 and extract a Trial Balance as on that date.

## 2.12 CONTROL ACCOUNTS

### Introduction

As the name implies, control accounts are used to verify the accuracy of the debtors and creditors ledgers, that is all credit transactions.
There are two important types of control accounts:

1. **Debtors Control Account** or **Sales Ledger Control Account** (a summary of all debtors accounts)
2. **Creditors Control Account** or **Purchases Ledger Control Account** (a summary of all creditors accounts)

### Uses of Control Accounts

(a) All details in the Debtors or Creditors Ledger are summarised in the respective control account. The total of the balances in the individual accounts should agree with the balance on the control account.
(b) They act as a check on the accuracy of the double-entry process. As a result any errors may be located more easily.
(c) Useful financial information is gained, such as the total amount due by the debtors and the total amount due to the creditors.

**Note** Control Accounts are **not** part of the double-entry process. Entries made in the control account will always be made on the same side as they appear in the debtors or creditors ledgers.

### *Example*

Write up the *Sales* and *Sales Returns Day Books,* post to the *ledgers,* and balance the accounts at the month end. Then draw up a *Debtors Control Account.*

| | |
|---|---|
| *Dec 1* | *Sold goods on credit to Agnew Ltd invoice No. 23 for IR£3,000* |
| *Dec 5* | *Agnew Ltd returned goods, sent credit note No. 2, IR£500* |
| *Dec 10* | *Sold goods on credit to Duff Ltd invoice No. 24 for IR£5,000* |
| *Dec 12* | *Received Cheque No. 123 from Agnew Ltd IR£1,000* |
| *Dec 18* | *Duff Ltd returned goods, sent credit note No. 3, IR£1,000* |
| *Dec 19* | *Duff Ltd paid IR£3,500 by cheque* |

SOLUTION

### *Day Books*

**Sales Day Book (1)**

| Date | Details | Inv. No. | Folio | Total |
|---|---|---|---|---|
| 1 Dec | Agnew Ltd | 23 | DL1 | 3,000 |
| 10 Dec | Duff Ltd | 24 | DL2 | 5,000 |
| | | | | 8,000 |
| | | | | (GL1) |

**Sales Returns Day Book (1)**

| Date | Details | C/N No. | Folio | Total |
|---|---|---|---|---|
| 5 Dec | Agnew Ltd | 2 | DL1 | 500 |
| 18 Dec | Duff Ltd | 3 | DL2 | 1,000 |
| | | | | 1,500 |
| | | | | (GL2) |

### *Cash Book*

**DR** **CR**

| Date | Details | F | Bank | Debtors | Date | Details | F | Bank |
|---|---|---|---|---|---|---|---|---|
| 12 Dec | Agnew Ltd | DL1 | 1,000 | 1,000 | 31 Dec | Balance | c/d | 4,500 |
| 19 Dec | Duff Ltd | DL2 | 3,500 | 3,500 | | | | |
| | | | 4,500 | 4,500 | | | | 4,500 |
| 31 Dec | Balance | b/d | 4,500 | | | | | |
| | | | (DL3) | | | | | |

## *General Ledger*

| Sales Account (1) | | | | | | | |
|---|---|---|---|---|---|---|---|
| | | | | 31 Dec | Total Sales | SDB1 | 8,000 |

| Sales Returns Account (2) | | | | | | | |
|---|---|---|---|---|---|---|---|
| 31 Dec | Total | SRDB1 | 1,500 | | | | |

## *Debtors Ledger*

| Agnew Account (1) | | | | | | | |
|---|---|---|---|---|---|---|---|
| 1 Dec | Credit Sales | SDB1 | 3,000 | 5 Dec | Sales Returns | SRDB1 | 500 |
| | | | | 18 Dec | Bank | CB | 1,000 |
| | | | | 31 Dec | Balance | c/d | 1,500 |
| | | | 3,000 | | | | 3,000 |
| 31 Dec | Balance | b/d | 1,500 | | | | |

| Duff Account (2) | | | | | | | |
|---|---|---|---|---|---|---|---|
| 10 Dec | Credit Sales | SDB1 | 5,000 | 18 Dec | Sales Returns | SRDB1 | 1,000 |
| | | | | 19 Dec | Bank | CB | 3,500 |
| | | | | 31 Dec | Balance | c/d | 500 |
| | | | 5,000 | | | | 5,000 |
| 31 Dec | Balance | b/d | 500 | | | | |

DR **Debtors Control Account (3)** CR

| Date | Details | F | IR£ | Date | Details | F | IR£ |
|---|---|---|---|---|---|---|---|
| 31 Dec | Sales | SDB1 | 8,000 | 31 Dec | Sales Returns | SRDB1 | 1,500 |
| | | | | | Cash | CB | 4,500 |
| | | | | | Balance | c/d | 2,000 |
| | | | 8,000 | | | | 8,000 |
| 31 Dec | Balance | b/d | 2,000 | | | | |

Extracted from the Sales Day Book

Extracted from the Sales Returns Day Book

Extracted from the Cash Book

**Note** The totals extracted from the Day Books and Cash Book are entered on the same side as they appear in the individual debtor's account

## Checking the Accuracy of the Accounts and the Double-Entry Process

| Individual Accounts | | Debtors Control Account | |
|---|---|---|---|
| Agnew Ltd | 1,500 | | |
| Duff Ltd | 500 | | |
| Total Debit Balances | 2,000 | Debit Balance | 2,000 |

From the above example, the total of the Debtor's individual balances agrees with the Closing Balance in the Debtors Control Account. Therefore it may be concluded that:

1. The total amount due by debtors is IR£2,000.
2. The Double-Entry process is accurate.

## Debtors Control Account (Sales Ledger Control Account)

The following is a summary of entries that should appear in the Debtors Control Account:

*Figure 2.9*

| DR Debtors Control Account | CR |
|---|---|
| (i) Balance at the beginning of the period | (iii) Sales Returns |
| (ii) Total Credit Sales | (iv) Payments made by Debtors |
| | (v) Closing Balance at the end of the period |

*(i) Balance at the beginning of the period*
The total amount due to the firm by all debtors at the start of the accounting period. This is found in the General Journal.

*(ii) Total Credit Sales*
The total amount of credit sales during the accounting period. This is found in the Sales Day Book.

*(iii) Sales Returns*
The total amount of sales returns during the accounting period. This is found in the Sales Returns Day Book.

*(iv) Payments made by Debtors*
This includes total cash and cheque payments received from the debtors during the accounting period. The total amount is found in the Cash Book.

*(v) Closing Balance at the end of the period*
This figure represents the total amount due by the debtors at the end of the accounting period. As noted earlier this balance should equal the total of the balances on the individual accounts in the Debtors Ledger.

An alternative format to the standard T-Account is also used. This is referred to as the **Continuous Balance Format**. The layout used is as below:

*Figure 2.10*

| Debtors Control Account | | | | |
|---|---|---|---|---|
| **Date** | **Details** | **DR** | **CR** | **Balance** |
| | | | | |

The following example will be worked through using both methods.

*Example*
Complete and balance the *Debtors Control Account* below, from the following information:

| | | IR£ |
|---|---|---|
| 1 May | Debtors Balance | 970 |
| | Total Credit Sales for May | 10,350 |
| | Total Cash received from Debtors | 9,780 |

(Junior Certificate Higher Level 1995, Paper I, Section A, Q3)

*T-Account Format (Given)*

| DR | | Debtors Control Account | | | CR |
|---|---|---|---|---|---|
| **Date** | **Details** | **IR£** | **Date** | **Details** | **IR£** |
| 1 May | Balance b/d | 970 | 31 May | Payments Received | 9,780 |
| 31 May | Total Credit Sales | 10,350 | 31 May | Balance c/d | 1,540 |
| | | 11,320 | | | 11,320 |
| 31 May | Balance b/d | 1,540 | | | |

The balance b/d of IR£1,540 (the total amount owed to the firm) should equal the total list of balances on the debtors' individual accounts in the Debtors Ledger.

*Continuous Balance Format*

| Debtors Control Account | | | | |
|---|---|---|---|---|
| **Date** | **Details** | **Debit** | **Credit** | **Balance** |
| 1 May | Opening Balance | | | 970 |
| 31 May | Total Credit Sales | 10,350 | | 11,320 |
| 31 May | Payments Received | | 9,780 | 1,540 |

## Exercises

1. Write up the *Sales Day Book* of Murray Ltd, post to the *ledgers*, and balance the accounts at the month end. Then draw up a *Debtors Control Account*. (All sales are on credit.)

   *Dec 3* *Sold goods to Brady Ltd invoice No. 43 for IR£5,000*
   *Dec 8* *Sold goods to Duffy Ltd invoice No. 44 for IR£3,000*
   *Dec 10* *Sold goods to Ellis Ltd invoice No. 45 for IR£7,000*
   *Dec 17* *Sold goods to Brady Ltd invoice No. 46 for IR£5,000*
   *Dec 21* *Sold goods to Ellis Ltd invoice No. 47 for IR£7,000*

2. Write up the *Sales Day Book* of Jones Ltd, post to the *ledgers*, and balance the accounts at the month end. Then draw up a *Debtors Control Account*. (All sales are on credit.)

   *Dec 5* *Sold goods to Murphy Ltd invoice No. 89 for IR£15,500*
   *Dec 9* *Sold goods to Ryan Ltd invoice No. 90 for IR£13,000*
   *Dec 19* *Sold goods to Tavey Ltd invoice No. 91 for IR£8,500*
   *Dec 20* *Sold goods to Murphy Ltd invoice No. 92 for IR£7,000*
   *Dec 21* *Ryan Ltd paid IR£13,000 by cheque*

3. Write up the *Sales Day Book* of Ward Ltd, post to the *ledgers*, and balance the accounts at the month end. Then draw up a *Debtors Control Account*. (All sales are on credit.)

   *Dec 1* *Sold goods to Collins Ltd invoice No. 77 for IR£8,500*
   *Dec 5* *Sold goods to Carey Ltd invoice No. 78 for IR£3,000*
   *Dec 10* *Collins Ltd returned goods, sent credit note No. 8, IR£500*
   *Dec 12* *Sold goods to Coffey Ltd invoice No. 79 for IR£3,800*
   *Dec 17* *Carey Ltd returned goods, sent credit note No. 9, IR£900*
   *Dec 20* *Coffey Ltd paid IR£3,000 by cheque*

4. From the following information, complete and balance the *Debtors Control Account* below in:

   (a) T-Account format
   (b) Continuous format

| | | IR£ |
|---|---|---|
| 1 Mar | Debtors Balance | 1,850 |
| | Total Credit Sales for March | 80,000 |
| | Total Cash received from Debtors in March | 64,000 |

**DR** **Debtors Control Account** **CR**

| Date | Details | IR£ | Date | Details | IR£ |
|---|---|---|---|---|---|
| | | | | | |

**Debtors Control Account**

| Date | Details | Debit | Credit | Balance |
|---|---|---|---|---|
| | | | | |

5. From the following information, complete and balance the *Debtors Control Account* below in:

   (a) T-Account format
   (b) Continuous format

| | | € |
|---|---|---|
| 1 Apr | Debtors Balance | 3,550 |
| | Total Credit Sales for March | 100,000 |
| | Total Cash received from Debtors in March | 88,000 |

**DR** **Debtors Control Account** **CR**

| Date | Details | € | Date | Details | € |
|---|---|---|---|---|---|
| | | | | | |

| Debtors Control Account | | | | |
|---|---|---|---|---|
| **Date** | **Details** | **Debit** | **Credit** | **Balance** |
| | | | | |

## Creditors Control Account (Purchases Ledger Control Account)

The following is a summary of entries that should appear in the Creditors Control Account:

*Figure 2.11*

| DR | Creditors Control Account CR |
|---|---|
| (iii) Purchases Returns<br>(iv) Payments made to Creditors<br>(v) Closing Balance at the end of the period | (i) Balance at the beginning of the period<br>(ii) Total Credit Purchases |

*(i) Balance at the beginning of the period*
The total amount due by the firm to all creditors at the start of the accounting period. This is found in the General Journal.

*(ii) Total Credit Purchases*
The total amount of credit purchases made during the accounting period. This is found in the Purchases Day Book.

*(iii) Purchases Returns*
The total amount of purchases returns during the accounting period. This is found in the Purchases Returns Day Book.

*(iv) Payments made to Creditors*
This includes total cash and cheque payments made to creditors during the accounting period. The total amount is found in the Cash Book.

*(v) Closing Balance at the end of the period*
This figure represents the total amount due to the creditors at the end of the accounting period. This balance should equal the total of the balances on the individual accounts in the Creditors Ledger.

As with the Debtors Control Account, both formats may be used. The following example will be worked through using both methods.

*Example*

Complete and balance the *Creditors Control Account* below, from the following data

| | | IR£ |
|---|---|---|
| 1 April | Creditors Balance | 2,620 |
| | Total Credit Purchases for April | 54,500 |
| | Total Payments (Cheque) during April | 46,300 |
| | Total Payments (Cash) during April | 380 |

(Junior Certificate (H.L) 1992, Paper I, Section A, Q4)

*SOLUTION*

*Continuous Balance Format (Given)*

| Creditors Control Account | | | | |
|---|---|---|---|---|
| **Date** | **Details** | **Debit** | **Credit** | **Balance** |
| 1 April | Opening Balance | | | 2,620 |
| 30 April | Total Credit Purchases | | 54,500 | 57,120 |
| 30 April | Payments Made (Cheque) | 46,300 | | 10,820 |
| 30 April | Payments Made (Cash) | 380 | | 10,440 |

*T-Account Format*

**DR** **Creditors Control Account** **CR**

| Date | Details | IR£ | Date | Details | IR£ |
|---|---|---|---|---|---|
| 30 April | Payments Made (Chqs) | 46,300 | 1 April | Balance b/d | 2,620 |
| 30 April | Payments Made (Cash) | 380 | 30 April | Total Credit Purchase | 54,500 |
| 30 April | Balance c/d | 10,440 | | | |
| | | 57,120 | | | 57,120 |
| | | | 30 April | Balance b/d | 10,440 |

The balance b/d of IR£10,440 (the total amount owed by the firm) should equal the total list of balances on the creditors individual accounts in the Creditors Ledger.

## Exercises

1. Write up the *Purchases Day Book* of Hogan Ltd, post to the *ledgers*, and balance the accounts at the month end. Then draw up a *Creditors Control Account.* (All purchases are on credit.)

   *May 3 Purchased goods from Hickey Ltd invoice No. 10 for IR£2,500*
   *May 8 Purchased goods from Hughes Ltd invoice No. 11 for IR£3,000*

*May10 Purchased goods from Howell Ltd invoice No. 12 for IR£6,600*
*May17 Purchased goods from Hickey Ltd invoice No. 13 for IR£4,400*
*May21 Purchased goods from Howell Ltd invoice No. 14 for IR£6,800*

2. Write up the *Purchases Day Book* of Jacobs Ltd, post to the *ledgers*, and balance the accounts at the month end. Then draw up a *Creditors Control Account*. (All purchases are on credit.)

    *Dec 7 Purchased goods from Power Ltd invoice No. 52 for IR£12,500*
    *Dec 8 Purchased goods from Regan Ltd invoice No. 53 for IR£8,500*
    *Dec 12 Purchased goods from Power Ltd invoice No. 54 for IR£9,500*
    *Dec 18 Purchased goods from Smyth Ltd invoice No. 55 for IR£12,000*
    *Dec 20 Paid IR£8,500 by cheque to Regan Ltd*

3. Write up the *Purchases Day Book* of Walshe Ltd, post to the *ledgers*, and balance the accounts at the month end. Then draw up a *Creditors Control Account*. (All purchases are on credit.)

    *Jun 1 Purchased goods from Gavin Ltd invoice No. 88 for IR£5,500*
    *Jun 5 Purchased goods from Flynn Ltd invoice No. 89 for IR£3,500*
    *Jun 10 Returned goods to Gavin Ltd received credit note No. 8, IR£1,500*
    *Jun 12 Purchased goods from Dennis Ltd invoice No. 90 for IR£7,800*
    *Jun 17 Returned goods to Dennis Ltd received credit note No. 9, IR£800*
    *Jun 20 Paid IR£3,000 by cheque to Gavin Ltd*

4. From the following information, complete and balance the Creditors Control Account below in:

    (a) T-Account format
    (b) Continuous format

| | | IR£ |
|---|---|---|
| 1 May | Creditors Balance | 5,550 |
| | Total credit purchases for May | 54,000 |
| | Total cheque payments to Creditors in May | 50,500 |

**DR** **Creditors Control Account** **CR**

| Date | Details | IR£ | Date | Details | IR£ |
|---|---|---|---|---|---|
| | | | | | |

| Creditors Control Account | | | | |
|---|---|---|---|---|
| Date | Details | Debit | Credit | Balance |
| | | | | |

5. From the following information, complete and balance the Creditors' Control Account below in:

   (a) T-Account format
   (b) Continuous format

| | | € |
|---|---|---|
| 1 Apr | Creditors Balance | 3,390 |
| | Total credit purchases during April | 78,000 |
| | Total cheque payments to Creditors in April | 88,000 |
| | Cash purchases during April | 5,000 |

**DR** **Creditors Control Account** **CR**

| Date | Details | € | Date | Details | € |
|---|---|---|---|---|---|
| | | | | | |

| Creditors Control Account | | | | |
|---|---|---|---|---|
| Date | Details | Debit | Credit | Balance |
| | | | | |

# CHAPTER 3
# CLUB ACCOUNTS

## Introduction

One of the main aims of a firm's existence is to maximise its profits. However some organisations are non-profit making and are formed for other reasons (e.g. to provide sporting facilities for the benefit of its members). Such organisations are called **clubs**. Accounts need to be prepared for the members in order to show how income is generated and subsequently spent.

The Treasurer is one of the club's officers, elected by the members at the Annual General Meeting (AGM), whose duties include the preparation of accounts. Other officers elected at the AGM are the Chairperson and Secretary.

## Role of Officers

*The Role of the Treasurer*

- Collecting the members' subscriptions, other donations, grants etc.
- Completing transactions with the bank, including lodging receipts and making payments by cheque or otherwise.
- Keeping financial records.
- Preparing the Final Accounts
  - (i) Receipts and Payments Account
  - (ii) Income and Expenditure Account
  - (iii) Balance Sheet
- Presenting the Treasurer's Report and Accounts at the AGM

*The Treasurer's Report should include:*

- The Final Accounts outlined above
- A statement on the financial affairs of the club including any recommendations regarding an increase in subscriptions or suggestions how future developments may be financed

*The Role of the Chairperson*

- He/she chairs the meetings, keeps order, follows the agenda and is responsible for the club's success

*The Role of the Secretary*

- Sends a notice and agenda of meetings to the members
- Arranges the meeting and records the minutes of all meetings
- Presents the Secretary's Report at the AGM

*Example*

You are the Secretary of the Castle Cricket Club. The Annual General Meeting will be held in the Pavilion Hotel, Castleblayney on January 31st 1999 at 8.00 p.m.

Required: Draft a suitable notice of meeting and agenda to send to all members.

*Figure 3.1*

**Notice of Meeting**

The Annual General Meeting of the Castle Cricket Club will be held in the Pavilion Hotel, Castleblayney on January 31st 1999 at 8.00 p.m.

David Davidson
Secretary

**Agenda**

1. Minutes of previous meeting
2. Matters arising
3. Secretary's Report
4. Treasurer's Report
5. Election of Officers
   - Chairperson
   - Secretary
   - Treasurer
6. AOB

## Terms Used in the Accounts

The accounts maintained by the club are similar to those kept by a firm. However, there are different terms used, these are summarised below:

*Figure 3.2*

| CLUB | FIRM / COMPANY |
|---|---|
| Receipts and Payments Account | Cash Book |
| Income and Expenditure Account | Profit and Loss Account |
| Accumulated Fund | Capital |
| Excess Income over Expenditure | Net Profit |
| Excess Expenditure over Income | Net Loss |
| Balance Sheet | Balance Sheet |

## 3.1 RECEIPTS AND PAYMENTS BOOK

As outlined above, this is similar in its operation to the Cash Book of a firm. It is a summary of all receipts and payments made over a particular period of time.

- Receipts are recorded on the debit side.
- Payments made are recorded on the credit side.
- Also included are the opening and closing balances.
- A debit Opening Balance indicates that the club has a sum of money in cash or alternatively in the bank.
- A credit Opening Balance represents a bank overdraft.
- An analysis of this account allows all interested parties to appreciate where money came from and where it was spent.

| (Debit) | **Receipts and Payments Account** | (Credit) |
|---|---|---|
| Receipts | | Payments |

***Example***

From the following details prepare a *Receipts and Payments Account* for the Castle Cricket Club for December 1999.

| *Dec* | | *IR£* |
|---|---|---|
| *01* | *Cash in bank* | *700* |
| *02* | *Purchase of Minerals* | *150* |
| *04* | *Membership Subscriptions* | *950* |
| *05* | *Caretaker's Wages* | *180* |
| *07* | *Sale of Minerals* | *220* |
| *08* | *Raffle Expenses* | *100* |
| *10* | *Raffle Receipts* | *150* |
| *14* | *Printing of tickets for Disco* | *50* |
| *15* | *Hire of Disc Jockey* | *110* |
| *19* | *Disco Tickets* | *300* |

*SOLUTION*

| Receipts and Payments Account of the Castle Cricket Club for December 1999 | | | | | |
|---|---|---|---|---|---|
| **Date** | **Details** | **Total** | **Date** | **Details** | **Total** |
| 1999 | | IR£ | 1999 | | IR£ |
| Dec 01 | Balance b/d | 700 | Dec 02 | Minerals | 150 |
| Dec 04 | Members' Subscriptions | 950 | Dec 05 | Caretaker's Wages | 180 |
| Dec 07 | Mineral Sales | 220 | Dec 08 | Raffle Expenses | 100 |
| Dec 10 | Raffle Receipts | 150 | Dec 14 | Printing of Tickets | 50 |
| Dec 19 | Disco Tickets | 300 | Dec 15 | Hire of Disc Jockey | 110 |
| | | | Dec 31 | Balance c/d | 1,730 |
| | | 2,320 | | | 2,320 |
| Jan 01 | Balance b/d | 1,730 | | | |

## Practice Questions

1. The Oval Rugby Club provided you with the following receipts and payments for the year ended 31 Dec 1999. At the beginning of the year there was IR£780 in the Bank. Prepare the Receipts and Payments Account.

| **Receipts:** | **IR£** |
|---|---|
| Membership subscriptions | 5,500 |
| Charity match proceeds | 2,500 |
| Refreshments | 1,500 |

| **Payments:** | **IR£** |
|---|---|
| Hire of bus | 700 |
| Program printing | 1,000 |
| Rugby balls | 200 |
| Refreshments | 1,200 |
| Donation to charity | 3,000 |
| Light and Heat | 1,100 |
| Insurance | 2,000 |

2. The Round Tennis Club provided you with the following receipts and payments for the year ended 31 Dec 2001. At the beginning of the year there was IR£180 in the Bank. Prepare the Receipts and Payments Account.

| **Receipts:** | **IR£** |
|---|---|
| Membership subscriptions | 3,500 |
| Disco receipts | 900 |
| Donation | 1,000 |

| **Payments:** | **IR£** |
|---|---|
| Tennis balls | 500 |
| Disco expenses | 1,200 |
| Light and Heat | 2,800 |

3. The Dimple Golf Club provided you with the following receipts and payments for the year ended 31.12.03. At the beginning of the year there was a bank overdraft of €300. Prepare the Receipts and Payments Account.

| **Receipts:** | **€** |
|---|---|
| Members' subscriptions | 9,500 |
| Green fees | 900 |

| **Payments:** | **€** |
|---|---|
| Wages | 7,500 |
| Insurance | 1,200 |
| Advertising | 2,800 |

## 3.2 ANALYSED RECEIPTS AND PAYMENTS BOOK

Using the same information given in the previous example prepare an Analysed Receipts and Payments Account under the following headings:

**Receipts (Debit):** Total, Minerals, Raffle, Disco and Other
**Payments (Credit):** Total, Minerals, Raffle, Disco and Other

*SOLUTION*

***Debit Side***

| **Receipts and Payments Account of the Castle Cricket Club for December 1999** | | | | | | |
|---|---|---|---|---|---|---|
| **Date** | **Details** | **Total** | **Minerals** | **Raffle** | **Disco** | **Other** |
| 1999 | | IR£ | IR£ | IR£ | IR£ | IR£ |
| Dec 01 | Balance b/d | 700 | | | | |
| Dec 04 | Membership Subscriptions | 950 | | | | 950 |
| Dec 07 | Mineral Sales | 220 | 220 | | | |
| Dec 10 | Raffle Receipts | 150 | | 150 | | |
| Dec 19 | Disco Tickets | 300 | | | 300 | |
| | | 2,320 | 220 | 150 | 300 | 950 |
| Jan 01 | Balance b/d | 1,730 | | | | |

*Credit Side*

| Receipts and Payments Account of the Castle Cricket Club for December 1999 | | | | | | |
|---|---|---|---|---|---|---|
| **Date** | **Details** | **Total** | **Minerals** | **Raffle** | **Disco** | **Other** |
| 1999 | | IR£ | IR£ | IR£ | IR£ | IR£ |
| Dec 02 | Minerals | 150 | 150 | | | |
| Dec 05 | Caretaker's Wages | 180 | | | | 180 |
| Dec 08 | Raffle Expenses | 100 | | 100 | | |
| Dec 14 | Printing of Tickets | 50 | | | 50 | |
| Dec 15 | Hire of Disc Jockey | 110 | | | 110 | |
| Dec 31 | Balance c/d | 1,730 | | | | |
| | | 2,320 | 150 | 100 | 160 | 180 |

**Note** *From the above example it may be seen that:*

- *The Opening and Closing Bank and/or Cash balances are never analysed*
- *The Analysis columns are totalled on each side but not made to balance*
- *Only the Bank and/or Cash column is balanced*

## Practice Questions

1. From the following details prepare an *Analysed Receipts and Payments Account* for Muckno Golf Club for Nov 99 under the following headings:

**Receipts (Debit):** Total, Green Fees, Subscriptions, Minerals, Other
**Payments (Credit):** Total, Minerals, Wages, Repairs, Other

| *Nov* | | *IR£* |
|---|---|---|
| *01* | *Cash in bank* | *850* |
| *02* | *Green fees received* | *950* |
| *04* | *Membership Subscriptions* | *550* |
| *05* | *Greenkeeper's Wages* | *280* |
| *09* | *Sale of Minerals* | *120* |
| *09* | *Raffle Receipts* | *50* |
| *11* | *Raffle Expenses* | *45* |
| *13* | *Repairs to Lawnmower* | *350* |
| *16* | *Secretary's Wages* | *270* |
| *19* | *Green fees received* | *700* |
| *20* | *Repairs to Clubhouse* | *800* |
| *22* | *Subscriptions received* | *200* |
| *27* | *Sale of Minerals* | *50* |
| *28* | *Purchased new Flag Pins* | *300* |
| *30* | *Purchased Minerals* | *220* |

2. From the following details prepare an *Analysed Receipts and Payments Account* for Lough Ski Club for May 2000 under the following headings:

   **Receipts (Debit):** Total, Subscriptions, Lessons, Other
   **Payments (Credit):** Total, Wages, Repairs, Petrol, Insurance, Other

| *May* | | *IR£* |
|---|---|---|
| *02* | *Cash on hand* | *300* |
| *04* | *Lesson receipts* | *450* |
| *04* | *Membership Subscriptions* | *205* |
| *05* | *Wages* | *175* |
| *07* | *Boat Repairs* | *115* |
| *09* | *Competition Receipts* | *150* |
| *12* | *Competition Expenses* | *95* |
| *17* | *Petrol* | *280* |
| *18* | *Wages* | *170* |
| *19* | *Lesson receipts* | *400* |
| *20* | *Repairs to Boathouse* | *100* |
| *22* | *Subscriptions received* | *150* |
| *27* | *Sale of Boat* | *750* |
| *28* | *Paid Insurance* | *300* |

3. From the following details prepare an *Analysed Receipts and Payments Account* for the local Draughts and Bridge Club for June 2002. Use the following analysis column headings:

   **Receipts (Debit):** Total, Subscriptions, Competition, Other
   **Payments (Credit):** Total, Competition, Rent, Light and Heat, Insurance, Other

| *June* | | **€** |
|---|---|---|
| *01* | *Bank Overdraft* | *95* |
| *02* | *Membership Subscriptions* | *115* |
| *03* | *Competition Entry Fees* | *35* |
| *04* | *Rent* | *75* |
| *06* | *ESB* | *25* |
| *09* | *Competition Receipts* | *50* |
| *10* | *Competition Expenses* | *35* |
| *12* | *Insurance* | *180* |
| *14* | *Heating Oil* | *65* |
| *19* | *Competition Receipts* | *100* |
| *20* | *Paid Insurance* | *20* |
| *21* | *Subscriptions received* | *150* |
| *22* | *Sale of old tables* | *50* |
| *23* | *Bought Light Bulbs* | *15* |
| *27* | *Bought Playing Cards* | *52* |
| *25* | *Prizes for the Competition* | *85* |

## 3.3 INCOME AND EXPENDITURE ACCOUNT

This account is similar in its operation to the Profit and Loss Account of a firm and contains the following information:

- Income received during the year. (e.g. Subscriptions, grants)
- Income due at the end of the year is added. (e.g. Subscriptions due)
- Income prepaid at the end of the year is subtracted. (e.g. Subscriptions prepaid)
- Expenses paid during the year (e.g. Wages)
- Expenses due at the end of the year are added. (e.g. Wages due)
- Expenses prepaid at the end of the year are subtracted. (e.g. Wages prepaid)
- A profit is referred to as an **excess of income over expenditure** (surplus)
- A loss is referred to as an **excess of expenditure over income** (deficit)

It should be noted that the Income and Expenditure Account does not take into account the following:

- Opening and closing cash/bank balances
- The purchase and/or sale of fixed assets

*Example*

From the following Receipts and Payments Account prepare an *Income and Expenditure Account* for the Castle Cricket Club for February 2000:

| Receipts and Payments Account of the Castle Cricket Club for February 2000 | | | | | |
|---|---|---|---|---|---|
| **Date** | **Details** | **Total** | **Date** | **Details** | **Total** |
| | | IR£ | | | IR£ |
| Feb 01 | Balance b/d | 980 | Feb 02 | Purchase of Lawnmower | 1,150 |
| Feb 04 | Membership Subscriptions | 1,500 | Feb 08 | Caretaker's Wages | 300 |
| Feb 19 | Catering Receipts | 320 | Feb 15 | Catering Expenses | 100 |
| | | | Feb 24 | Advertising | 150 |
| | | | Feb 29 | Balance c/d | 1,100 |
| | | 2,800 | | | 2,800 |
| Mar 01 | Balance b/d | 1,100 | | | |

*SOLUTION*

| Income and Expenditure Account of the Castle Cricket Club for February 2000 | | |
|---|---|---|
| | IR£ | IR£ |
| **Income** | | |
| Membership Subscriptions | 1,500 | |
| Catering Profit (320–100) | 220 | |
| | | 1,720 |
| **Expenditure** | | |
| Caretaker's Wages | 300 | |
| Advertising | 150 | |
| | | 450 |
| **Excess Income over Expenditure** | | 1,270 |

**Note** *From the above example it may be seen that:*

- *The opening bank balance and closing bank balance (Current Asset ➔ Balance Sheet) and the purchase of lawnmower (Fixed Asset ➔ Balance Sheet) are not included*
- *It is normal practice to net the catering receipts and expenses and then insert the resulting profit or loss in Income or Expenditure respectively. Other examples that may be treated in the same manner include dance receipts and expenditure, competition receipts and expenditure, and raffle receipts and expenditure*

## Practice Questions

1. From the following Receipts and Payments Account prepare an *Income and Expenditure Account* for the Counsel Cricket Club for May 2000.

| Receipts and Payments Account of the Counsel Cricket Club for May 2000 | | | | | |
|---|---|---|---|---|---|
| **Date** | **Details** | **Total** | **Date** | **Details** | **Total** |
| | | IR£ | | | IR£ |
| May 01 | Balance b/d | 300 | May 03 | Purchase of Tractor | 6,000 |
| May 05 | Membership Subscriptions | 8,500 | May 09 | Groundsman's Wages | 800 |
| May 21 | Catering Receipts | 400 | May 17 | Catering Expenses | 300 |
| | | | May 24 | Insurance | 2,000 |
| | | | May 31 | Balance c/d | 100 |
| | | 9,200 | | | 9,200 |
| Jun 01 | Balance b/d | 100 | | | |

2. From the following Receipts and Payments Account prepare an *Income and Expenditure Account* for the Young Youth Club for December 2001.

| Receipts and Payments Account of the Young Youth Club for December 2001 | | | | | |
|---|---|---|---|---|---|
| **Date** | **Details** | **Total** | **Date** | **Details** | **Total** |
| | | IR£ | | | IR£ |
| Dec 01 | Balance b/d | 150 | Dec 03 | Purchases of Tuck | 400 |
| Dec 07 | Tuck Shop Receipts | 500 | Dec 08 | Rent of Hall | 200 |
| Dec 20 | Annual Subscriptions | 250 | Dec 18 | Heat and Light | 100 |
| | | | Dec 19 | Insurance | 150 |
| | | | Dec 31 | Balance c/d | 50 |
| | | 900 | | | 900 |
| Jan 01 | Balance b/d | 50 | | | |

3. From the following Receipts and Payments Account prepare an *Income and Expenditure Account* for the Golden Oldies Club for March 2003.

| Receipts and Payments Account of the Golden Oldies Club for March 2003 | | | | | |
|---|---|---|---|---|---|
| **Date** | **Details** | **Total** | **Date** | **Details** | **Total** |
| | | € | | | € |
| Mar 02 | Membership Subscriptions | 1,000 | Mar 01 | Balance b/d | 500 |
| Mar 09 | Bingo Receipts | 340 | Mar 09 | Light and Heat | 80 |
| Mar 11 | Donation | 60 | Mar 17 | Bingo Prizes | 150 |
| | | | Mar 24 | Insurance | 200 |
| | | | Mar 28 | Rent | 135 |
| | | | Mar 31 | Balance c/d | 335 |
| | | 1,400 | | | 1,400 |
| Apr 01 | Balance b/d | 335 | | | |

**INCOME AND EXPENDITURE ACCOUNT including adjustments**

The income and expenditure account reveals the true financial position of the club. The receipts and payments account may reveal a positive bank balance. However the income and expenditure account may show an excess of expenditure over income. Adjustments such as expenses due (e.g. wages due) or revenues prepaid (e.g. subscriptions prepaid) may account for this.

## Main Adjustments

*(A) Subscriptions Due/Prepaid*

Members normally pay an annual fee to a club or society to avail themselves of its facilities. These subscriptions are the main source of income for a club. They are treated as income in the Income and Expenditure Account for the appropriate accounting period. Some members may have paid their membership in advance or the more likely scenario is that subscriptions are owed.

Treatment is summarised as follows:

*Figure 3.3*

| Income and Expenditure Account | Source of figure |
|---|---|
| Subscriptions received | Receipts and Payments Account<br>Or<br>Trial Balance |
| **ADD** Subscriptions due at year-end | Notes to the Accounts |
| **LESS** Subscriptions prepaid at year-end | Notes to the Accounts |
| **EQUALS** Subscriptions | **Final amount for Income and Expenditure a/c.** |

| Balance Sheet | |
|---|---|
| Subscriptions due at year-end ➔ | Current Asset |
| Subscriptions prepaid at year-end ➔ | Current Liability |

*(B) Expenses Due/Prepaid*

At the end of the accounting period some expenses may be still owed for that period. These are treated as expenditure in the Income and Expenditure account. On the other hand some expenses may have been paid for the next accounting period. These must be excluded from the expense in the income and expenditure account.

Treatment is summarised as follows:

*Figure 3.4*

| Income and Expenditure Account | Source of figure |
|---|---|
| Expense paid | Receipts and Payments Account<br>Or<br>Trial Balance |
| **ADD** Expense due at year-end | Notes to the Accounts |
| **LESS** Expense prepaid at year-end | Notes to the Accounts |
| **EQUALS** Expense | **Final amount for Income and Expenditure a/c.** |

| Balance Sheet | |
|---|---|
| Expenses due at year-end ➔ | Current Liability |
| Expenses prepaid at year-end ➔ | Current Asset |

### *(C) Depreciation*

Depreciation is treated as a running expense of the club and is included as expenditure in the Income and Expenditure account. Fixed assets are reduced in value by way of depreciation in order to reflect wear and tear or obsolescence.

After calculation of the percentage depreciation, it is treated as follows:

*Figure 3.5*

| Income and Expenditure Account | Source of figure |
|---|---|
| Depreciation | Notes to the Accounts<br>(The actual amount is normally calculated as a percentage) |

| Balance Sheet | Cost | Depreciation | Net Book Value |
|---|---|---|---|
| Fixed Asset | xxxxx | xxxxx | xxxxx |
| | (1) | (2) | (1) minus (2) |

### *(D) Trading Account*

As in any firm, a club must also prepare a trading account where opening and/or closing stocks exist. In general it is required to prepare a trading account for the bar or sale of minerals where sales, purchases, opening and/or closing stocks are given.

*Figure 3.6 — Layout of a typical Trading Account*

| Bar Trading Account | | |
|---|---|---|
| Sales (Bar Receipts) | | xxxxx |
| Opening Stock | xxxxx | |
| Add Purchases (Bar Purchases) | xxxxx | |
| | xxxxx | xxxxx |
| Less Closing Stock | xxxxx | xxxxx |
| Cost of Sales | | xxxxx |
| Bar Profit/Loss | | xxxxx |

The figure for the bar profit is transferred to the income section of the Income and Expenditure Account. Similarly a loss is treated as expenditure in the expenditure section of the Income and Expenditure Account. The closing stock figure is a balance sheet item as it is a current asset of the club.

*Example including adjustments*

The example below is similar to a previous one except for two additional pieces of information or adjustments.

From the following Receipts and Payments Account prepare an *Income and Expenditure Account* for the Castle Cricket Club for February 2000.

| Receipts and Payments Account of the Castle Cricket Club for February 2000 | | | | | |
|---|---|---|---|---|---|
| **Date** | **Details** | **Total** | **Date** | **Details** | **Total** |
| | | IR£ | | | IR£ |
| Feb 01 | Balance b/d | 980 | Feb 02 | Purchase of Lawnmower | 1,150 |
| Feb 04 | Membership Subscriptions | 1,500 | Feb 08 | Caretaker's Wages | 300 |
| Feb 19 | Catering Receipts | 320 | Feb 15 | Catering Expenses | 100 |
| | | | Feb 24 | Advertising | 150 |
| | | | Feb 29 | Balance c/d | 1,100 |
| | | 2,800 | | | 2,800 |
| Mar 01 | Balance b/d | 1,100 | | | |

**Notes** On 29.2.00

(a) Caretaker's wages due IR£100
(b) Subscriptions prepaid IR£600

*SOLUTION*

| Income and Expenditure Account of the Castle Cricket Club for February 2000 | | | |
|---|---|---|---|
| | **IR£** | **IR£** | **IR£** |
| **Income** | | | |
| Membership Subscriptions | 1,500 | | |
| Less Subscriptions prepaid | 600 | 900 | |
| Catering Profit | | 220 | |
| | | | 1,120 |

| Income and Expenditure Account of the Castle Cricket Club for February 2000 *contd.* | | | |
|---|---|---|---|
| **Expenditure** | | | |
| Caretaker's Wages | 300 | | |
| Add Wages Due | 100 | 400 | |
| Advertising | | 150 | |
| | | | 550 |
| **Excess Income over Expenditure** | | | 570 |

**Note** *From the above example it may be seen that:*

- *Subscriptions prepaid reduce the actual amount received by IR£600. Therefore the club owes its members IR£600 and this is recorded in the Balance Sheet as a Current Liability.*
- *Wages due increase the actual amount owed by IR£100. Therefore the club owes its caretaker IR£100 and this is recorded in the Balance Sheet as a Current Liability.*

**COMBINATION QUESTIONS at the end of the chapter**

### *Example including adjustments and Trading Account*

From the following Receipts and Payments Account prepare an *Income and Expenditure Account* for the Castle Cricket Club for February 2000.

| Receipts and Payments Account of the Castle Cricket Club for February 2000 | | | | | |
|---|---|---|---|---|---|
| **Date** | **Details** | **Total** | **Date** | **Details** | **Total** |
| | IR£ | | | IR£ | |
| Feb 01 | Balance b/d | 980 | Feb 02 | Purchase of Lawnmower | 1,150 |
| Feb 04 | Membership Subscriptions | 1,500 | Feb 08 | Caretaker's Wages | 300 |
| Feb 19 | Catering Receipts | 320 | Feb 15 | Catering Expenses | 100 |
| Feb 28 | Bar receipts | 1,250 | Feb 24 | Advertising | 150 |
| | | | Feb 28 | Bar Purchases | 770 |
| | | | Feb 29 | Balance c/d | 1,580 |
| | | 4,050 | | | 4,050 |
| Mar 01 | Balance b/d | 1,580 | | | |

**Notes** On 29.2.00

| | | | |
|---|---|---|---|
| (a) | Caretaker's wages due | | IR£100 |
| (b) | Subscriptions prepaid | | IR£600 |
| (c) | Bar Stock | 1.2.00 | IR£455 |
| | | 29.2.00 | IR£555 |

*SOLUTION*

The Trading Account must be prepared separately to the Income and Expenditure Account. It is similar in layout to that of a firm.

| Bar Trading Account of the Castle Cricket Club for February 2000 | | |
|---|---|---|
| | IR£ | IR£ |
| Sales (Bar Receipts) | | 1,250 |
| Less Cost of Sales | | |
| Opening Stock | 455 | |
| Add Purchases | 770 | |
| | 1,225 | |
| Less Closing Stock | 555 | |
| Cost of Sales | | 670 |
| **Bar Profit** | | 580 |

| Income and Expenditure Account of the Castle Cricket Club for February 2000 | | |
|---|---|---|
| | IR£ | IR£ |
| **Income** | | |
| Bar Profit | 580 | |
| Membership Subscriptions (1,500 – 600) | 900 | |
| Catering Profit | 220 | |
| | | 1,700 |
| **Expenditure** | | |
| Caretaker's Wages (300 + 100) | 400 | |
| Advertising | 150 | |
| | | 550 |
| **Excess Income over Expenditure** | | 1,150 |

**COMBINATION QUESTIONS at the end of the chapter**

## 3.4 BALANCE SHEET

This final account is the same as the balance sheet of a sole trader/firm. However the following should be noted:

- The term capital is not used. In club accounts the capital is referred to as the **Accumulated Fund.** Should you be required to calculate the Accumulated Fund, the following approach should be adopted:

Accumulated Fund = Assets – Liabilities

Step 1: Find the total **assets** at the **beginning** of the accounting period

Step 2: Find the total **liabilities** at the **beginning** of the accounting period

Step 3: **Subtract** the total liabilities from the total assets

- In all balance sheets completed to date, net profit has been added to the capital and a net loss has been subtracted. In club accounts an excess of income over expenditure is added to the accumulated fund and an excess of expenditure over income is subtracted.

## Comprehensive Example

The Treasurer of the local Social Club has been taken ill and you have been asked to prepare accounts for the Annual General Meeting next week. You are required to prepare:

- An *Income and Expenditure Account* for the year ended 31.5.92
- A separate *Trading Account* for the same period
- A *Balance Sheet* as at 31.5.92.

The Trial Balance at 31.5.92 is as shown:

| **Trial Balance as at 31.5.92** | **DR** | **CR** |
|---|---|---|
| | **IR£** | **IR£** |
| Clubhouse | 15,000 | |
| Equipment | 4,200 | |
| Canteen Sales | | 8,500 |
| Membership Subscriptions | | 4,600 |
| Canteen Purchases | 6,850 | |
| Light and Heat | 800 | |
| Telephone | 350 | |
| Postage and Stationery | 70 | |
| Wages | 3,200 | |
| Repairs to Equipment | 530 | |
| Furniture | 2,500 | |
| Profit on raffle | | 900 |
| Canteen Stock (1.6.91) | 440 | |
| Accumulated Fund (1.6.91) | | 19,940 |
| | 33,940 | 33,940 |

The following matters must also be taken into consideration:

| | | |
|---|---|---|
| *(i) Subscriptions due* | | *IR£310* |
| *(ii) Canteen Stock (31.5.92)* | | *IR£490* |
| *(iii) Telephone due* | | *IR£40* |
| *(iv) Depreciate* | *equipment by* | *10%* |
| | *furniture by* | *5%* |

(Junior Certificate 1992 Higher Level, PI, Section B, Q6a)

*SOLUTION*

(Hint: The question asks for the Income and Expenditure Account first. However, we need to find the canteen Profit/Loss, therefore it is suggested that the canteen Trading Account should be attempted before the Income and Expenditure Account)

| Canteen Trading Account for the local Social Club for the year ended 31.5.92 | | |
|---|---|---|
| | IR£ | IR£ |
| Sales (Canteen) | | 8,500 |
| Less Cost of Sales | | |
| Opening Stock(1.6.91) | 440 | |
| Add Purchases | 6,850 | |
| | 7,290 | |
| Less Closing Stock (31.5.92) | 490 | |
| Cost of Sales | | 6,800 |
| **Canteen Profit** | | 1,700 |

| Income and Expenditure Account for the local Social Club for year ended 31.5.92 | | | |
|---|---|---|---|
| | IR£ | IR£ | IR£ |
| **Income** | | | |
| Membership Subscriptions | | 4,600 | |
| Add Subscriptions due | | 310 | 4,910 |
| Raffle Profit | | | 900 |
| Canteen Profit | | | 1,700 |
| | | | 7,510 |
| **Expenditure** | | | |
| Light and Heat | | 800 | |
| Telephone | 350 | | |
| Add Telephone due | 40 | 390 | |
| Postage and stationery | | 70 | |
| Wages | | 3,200 | |

| Income and Expenditure Account for the local Social Club for year ended 31.5.92 *contd.* | | | |
|---|---|---|---|
| Repairs | | 530 | |
| Depreciation: Equipment | | 420 | |
| Furniture | | 125 | 5,535 |
| **Excess Income over Expenditure** | | | 1,975 |

| Balance Sheet for the local Social Club as at 31.5.92 | | | |
|---|---|---|---|
| | **IR£** | **IR£** | **IR£** |
| **Fixed Assets** | Cost | Depreciation | NBV |
| Clubhouse | 15,000 | - | 15,000 |
| Equipment | 4,200 | 420 | 3,780 |
| Furniture | 2,500 | 125 | 2,375 |
| | 21,700 | 545 | 21,155 |
| **Current Assets** | | | |
| Canteen Stock | | 490 | |
| Subscriptions due | | 310 | |
| | | 800 | |
| **Less Current Liabilities** | | | |
| Telephone due | | 40 | |
| Working Capital | | | 760 |
| Total Net Assets | | | 21,915 |
| **Financed by:** | | | |
| Accumulated Fund (1.6.91) | | | 19,940 |
| Add: Excess Income | | | 1,975 |
| | | | 21,915 |

## 3.5 COMBINATION QUESTIONS

1. The Treasurer of Cill Aodáin football club has prepared the following Receipts and Payments Account for the year ending 31.12.98.

| Details | Total | Details | Total |
|---|---|---|---|
| | IR£ | | IR£ |
| Subscriptions | 8,600 | 1.1.98 Balance b/d | 3,185 |
| Bar Sales | 58,350 | Rent | 2,400 |
| Raffle Income | 9,790 | Purchase of Bar Stock | 36,500 |
| Sale of Tractor | 6,670 | Insurance | 3,780 |
| | | Travel Expenses | 8,345 |

***contd.***

| Details | Total | Details | Total |
|---|---|---|---|
| | IR£ | | IR£ |
| | | Purchase of Equipment | 25,800 |
| | | Raffle Prizes | 2,800 |
| | | Balance c/d | 600 |
| | 83,410 | | 83,410 |
| Balance b/d | 600 | | |

The following information should also be taken into consideration on the 31.12.98.

*(i) Depreciate equipment by 12½% per annum*
*(ii) Subscriptions due IR£250*
*(iii) Rent Prepaid IR£370*
*(iv) Travel Expenses due IR£475*
*(v) Bar Stock on 1.1.98 IR£3,600*
*(vi) Bar Stock on 31.12.98 IR£4,100*

Prepare the:

(a) *Bar Trading Account*
(b) *Income and Expenditure Account* for the year ending 31.12.98

(Junior Certificate 1999 Higher Level, PI, Section B, Q5a)

2. Southern Shore Sailing Club has prepared the following Receipts and Payments Account for the year ending 31.12.97.

| Details | Total | Details | Total |
|---|---|---|---|
| | IR£ | | IR£ |
| 1.1.97 Balance | 15,176 | Purchase of Premises | 40,000 |
| Subscriptions | 9,300 | Instructors' Wages | 12,500 |
| Raffle Income | 7,198 | Telephone | 635 |
| Dinner Dance | 6,430 | Catering Expenses | 2,466 |
| Sale of Equipment | 17,500 | Insurance | 2,700 |
| 31.12.97 Balance | 4,294 | Light and Heat | 1,597 |
| | 59,898 | | 59,898 |

You are required to prepare the club's Income and Expenditure Account for the year ended 31.12.97 taking the following into consideration:

*(a) The club is owed IR£860 in respect of the dinner dance*
*(b) Subscriptions prepaid on 31.12.97 were IR£800*

*(c) Telephone bill due on 31.12.97 is IR£147*
*(d) Depreciation on premises is 2% per annum*

(Junior Certificate 1998 Higher Level, PI, Section B, Q3b)

3. Killinane Drama Society gives two public performances each year at Easter and November.

   On the 1st January 1996 it had an overdraft of IR£379 in the bank. The following extracts show the **totals** of the Cash Received and Lodgement Book and the Cheque Payments Book for the year ending 31.12.96.

**Analysed Cash Receipts and Lodgement Book (IR£)**

| Date | Particulars | Bank | Raffle | Concert | Refreshments | Subscriptions |
|---|---|---|---|---|---|---|
| 31.12.96 | Total | 3,637 | 933 | 2,057 | 247 | 400 |

**Analysed Cheque Payments Book (IR£)**

| Date | Particulars | Bank | Advertising | Refreshments | Rent | Travel | Equipment |
|---|---|---|---|---|---|---|---|
| 31.12.96 | Total | 2,641 | 193 | 152 | 340 | 156 | 1,800 |

The following additional information is available at the end of the financial year:

| | |
|---|---|
| *(i) Subscriptions due* | *IR£45* |
| *(ii) Rent due* | *IR£160* |
| *(iii) Advertising prepaid* | *IR£69* |

Assume you are the Treasurer finalising the accounts for the AGM
Prepare:

(a) A *Receipts and Payments Account*
(b) An *Income and Expenditure Account*

(Junior Certificate 1997, PI, Section B, Q3a)

4 The following information was presented by the Treasurer of Liosnacree Hurling Club for the year ending 31 December 1994.

| | |
|---|---|
| Cash in hand 1.1.94 | IR£430 |
| **Payments:** | **IR£** |
| Travel Expenses | 2,470 |
| Light and Heat | 520 |
| Insurance | 760 |
| Purchase of Lawnmower | 6,500 |
| Raffle Prizes | 580 |

| **Receipts:** | **IR£** |
|---|---|
| Membership Fees | 500 |
| Gate Receipts | 1,200 |
| Raffle Income | 7,600 |

Additional information:

*(i) Membership fees due on 31.12.94 IR£150*
*(ii) Insurance prepaid on 31.12.94 IR£140*
*(iii) Lawnmower to be depreciated by 10% each year*

Prepare:

(a) A *Receipts and Payments Account*
(b) An *Income and Expenditure Account* for the year ending 31.12.94 from the information above

(Junior Certificate 1995 Higher Level, PI, Section B, Q4a)

5. The Treasurer of Kileen G.A.A. Club has prepared the following Receipts and Payments Account for the year ending 31.12.93.

| Details | Total | Details | Total |
|---|---|---|---|
| | IR£ | | IR£ |
| 1.1.93 Balance b/f | 13,200 | Caretaker's Wages | 4,200 |
| Subscriptions | 3,300 | Travel Expenses | 2,910 |
| Bar Sales | 34,400 | Insurance | 1,290 |
| Gate Receipts | 4,250 | Bar Purchases | 30,150 |
| | | Secretary's Expenses | 850 |
| | | Purchase of Equipment | 9,800 |
| | | Balance c/d | 5,950 |
| | 55,150 | | 55,150 |
| 31.12.93 Balance b/d | 5,950 | | |

The following information should also be taken into consideration on the 31.12.93:

*(i) Subscriptions due IR£250*
*(ii) Insurance prepaid IR£250*
*(iii) Depreciation of equipment 10% per annum*
*(iv) Bar Stock on 1.1.93 IR£5,000*
*(v) Bar Stock on 31.12.93 IR£7,500*

Prepare:

(a) *Bar Trading Account*
(b) *Income and Expenditure Account* for the year ending 31.12.93

(Junior Certificate 1994 Higher Level, PI, Section B, Q6a)

6. The Ultrafit Aerobics Club has prepared its Receipts and Payments Account for the year ended 30.9.91.

| Details | Total | Details | Total |
|---|---|---|---|
| | IR£ | | IR£ |
| 1.10.90 Balance b/d | 400 | Affiliation Fees | 190 |
| Subscriptions | 2,500 | Rent of Premises | 1,600 |
| Fundraising | 800 | Admin. Expenses | 130 |
| Bar Sales | 1,260 | Fundraising Expenses | 210 |
| | | Purchase of Equipment | 670 |
| | | Bar Purchases | 890 |
| | | Balance c/d | 1,270 |
| | 4,960 | | 4,960 |

The following information should also be taken into consideration on the 30.9.91.

*(i) Subscriptions due* *IR£310*
*(ii) Rent on premises due* *IR£180*
*(iii) Depreciation of equipment 10% per annum*
*(iv) Bar Stock on 30.9.91* *IR£180*

Prepare:

(a) *Bar Trading Account*
(b) *Income and Expenditure Account* for the year ending 30.9.91

(Junior Certificate Sample Paper A, PI, Section B, Q4a)

# Chapter 4
# Service Firm Accounts

## Introduction

Firms or individuals that supply services, for example doctors, dentists, solicitors and accountants, keep accounts in order to:

- Calculate the profit or loss made
- Maintain records of monies due to and by the service firm
- Calculate tax liability due to the Revenue Commissioners
- Provide relevant financial information when applying for a loan

## Terms Used in the Accounts

The accounts that are maintained by service firms are similar to those kept by trading firms and clubs. However, there are some different terms used, these are summarised below:

*Figure 4.1*

| SERVICE FIRM | CLUB | FIRM / COMPANY |
|---|---|---|
| Analysed Cash Book | Receipts and Payments Account | Cash Book |
| Operating Statement | Income and Expenditure Account | Profit and Loss Account |
| Net Profit | Excess Income over Expenditure | Net Profit |
| Net Loss | Excess Expenditure over Income | Net Loss |
| Capital | Accumulated Fund | Capital |
| Balance Sheet | Balance Sheet | Balance Sheet |

## 4.1 ANALYSED CASH BOOK

As outlined in the previous chapter, the Analysed Cash Book is a normal T-Account with extra columns. These allow the service firm to identify where money is received from and what it is spent on.

- Receipts received are recorded on the DEBIT side
- Payments made are recorded on the CREDIT side
- Also included are the opening and closing balances
- A debit Opening/Closing Balance indicates that the service firm has a sum of money in cash or alternatively in the bank
- A credit Opening/ Closing Balance represents a bank overdraft

***Example***

Hehir Hair Ltd has three hairdressing salons in Co. Monaghan. From the following details record the transactions in the *Analysed Cash Book* for the month of August 1999 using the following headings:

**Debit Side:** Bank, Ballybay, Clones, Emyvale
**Credit Side:** Bank, Wages, Light and Heat, Insurance, Shampoo, Other

| | ***1999*** | | | | ***IR£*** |
|---|---|---|---|---|---|
| *Aug* | *01* | *Cash in bank* | | | *1,700* |
| | *02* | *Purchase of Shampoo* | | *(Cheque No. 4)* | *50* |
| | *06* | *ESB Bill* | | *(Cheque No. 5)* | *150* |
| | *08* | *Cleaner's Wages* | | *(Cheque No. 6)* | *180* |
| | *12* | *Customer Receipts* | *Ballybay* | | *220* |
| | | | *Clones* | | *350* |
| | | | *Emyvale* | | *210* |
| | *15* | *Wages* | | *(Cheque No. 7)* | *375* |
| | *18* | *Insurance* | | *(Cheque No. 8)* | *150* |
| | *20* | *Purchase of Shampoo* | | *(Cheque No. 9)* | *75* |
| | *30* | *Wages* | | *(Cheque No. 10)* | *570* |
| | *31* | *Customer Receipts* | *Ballybay* | | *320* |
| | | | *Clones* | | *550* |
| | | | *Emyvale* | | *330* |

*Solution*

***Debit Side***

| **Analysed Cash Book of Hehir Hair Ltd for the month of August 1999** | | | | | |
|---|---|---|---|---|---|
| **Date** | **Details** | **Bank** | **Ballybay** | **Clones** | **Emyvale** |
| 1999 | | IR£ | IR£ | IR£ | IR£ |
| Aug 01 | Balance b/d | 1,700 | | | |
| Aug 12 | Customer Receipts | 780 | 220 | 350 | 210 |
| Aug 31 | Customer Receipts | 1,200 | 320 | 550 | 330 |
| | | 3,680 | 540 | 900 | 540 |
| Sep 01 | Balance b/d | 2,130 | | | |

*Credit Side*

| Analysed Cash Book of Hehir Hair Ltd for the month of August 1999 | | | | | | | |
|---|---|---|---|---|---|---|---|
| **Date** | **Details** | **Cheque No.** | **Bank** | **Wages** | **Light/Heat** | **Insurance** | **Shampoo** |
| 1999 | | | IR£ | IR£ | IR£ | IR£ | IR£ |
| Aug 02 | Shampoo | 4 | 50 | | | | 50 |
| Aug 06 | ESB | 5 | 150 | | 150 | | |
| Aug 08 | Cleaner's Wages | 6 | 180 | 180 | | | |
| Aug 15 | Wages | 7 | 375 | 375 | | | |
| Aug 18 | Insurance | 8 | 150 | | | 150 | |
| Aug 20 | Shampoo | 9 | 75 | | | | 75 |
| Aug 30 | Wages | 10 | 570 | 570 | | | |
| Aug 31 | Balance c/d | | 2,130 | | | | |
| | | | 3,680 | 1,125 | 150 | 150 | 125 |

**Note** From the above example it may be seen that:

- ► The Opening and Closing Bank and/or Cash balances are never analysed
- ► The Analysis columns are totalled on each side but are not made to balance
- ► Only the Bank and/or Cash columns are balanced

## Practice Questions

1. Write up the *Analysed Cash Book* (Analysed Receipts and Payments Book) of Forde Ltd, a vehicles rental firm, for the month of July 1999 from the following information.

   Use the following money column headings:

   **Debit (Receipts) side:** Bank, Car, Van, Truck
   **Credit (Payments) side:** Bank, Wages, Fuel, Advertising, Other

| | | | ***IR£*** |
|---|---|---|---|
| *1.7.99* | *Cash in Bank* | | *3,330* |
| *3.7.99* | *Receipts from customers* | *Receipt No. 11* | |
| | *Car Rentals* | | *12,230* |
| | *Van Rentals* | | *8,880* |
| | *Truck Rentals* | | *6,790* |
| *5.7.99* | *Paid wages* | *Cheque No. 22* | *4,040* |
| *6.7.99* | *Paid advertising agency* | *Cheque No. 23* | *2,800* |
| *9.7.99* | *Purchased a car* | *Cheque No. 24* | *12,000* |
| *12.7.99* | *Paid for petrol* | *Cheque No. 25* | *3,090* |
| *14.7.99* | *Paid for diesel* | *Cheque No. 26* | *2,890* |
| *18.7.99* | *Paid insurance* | *Cheque No. 27* | *2,850* |
| *20.7.99* | *Paid wages* | *Cheque No. 28* | *3,800* |

| | | | |
|---|---|---|---|
| *21.7.99* | *Receipts from customers* | *Receipt No. 12* | |
| | *Car Rentals* | | *8,885* |
| | *Van Rentals* | | *7,775* |
| | *Truck Rentals* | | *3,690* |
| *25.7.99* | *Paid advertising* | *Cheque No. 29* | *1,000* |
| *28.7.99* | *Paid wages* | *Cheque No. 30* | *3,700* |
| *31.7.99* | *Paid for petrol* | *Cheque No. 31* | *2,500* |

2. Write up the *Analysed Cash Book* (Analysed Receipts and Payments Book) of Colette Cary, a dentist, for the month of July 2001 from the following information.

   Use the following money column headings:

   **Debit (Receipts) side:** Bank, Dental, Work, Dental Products, Other
   **Credit (Payments) side:** Bank, Telephone, Light and Heat, Rent, Other

| | | | ***IR£*** |
|---|---|---|---|
| *1.7.01* | *Bank Overdraft* | | *2,400* |
| *4.7.01* | *Receipts from customers* | *Receipt No. 18* | |
| | *Dental Work* | | *1,450* |
| | *Dental Products* | | *600* |
| *6.7.01* | *Paid telephone bill* | *Cheque No. 42* | *440* |
| *6.7.01* | *Paid ESB bill* | *Cheque No. 43* | *400* |
| *10.7.01* | *Purchased a new drill* | *Cheque No. 44* | *2,000* |
| *11.7.01* | *Paid rent* | *Cheque No. 45* | *150* |
| *14.7.01* | *Paid for heating oil* | *Cheque No. 46* | *290* |
| *19.7.01* | *Paid insurance* | *Cheque No. 47* | *850* |
| *20.7.01* | *Paid rent* | *Cheque No. 48* | *150* |
| *22.7.01* | *Receipts from customers* | *Receipt No. 19* | |
| | *Dental Work* | | *1,950* |
| | *Dental Products* | | *350* |
| *24.7.01* | *Paid Telecom* | *Cheque No. 49* | *500* |
| *28.7.01* | *Paid rent* | *Cheque No. 50* | *150* |
| *31.7.01* | *Received a bank loan* | *Receipt No. 20* | *3,000* |

3. Decor Ltd provides an interior design service. On 1 May 2005, the firm has €1,200 in the bank. The following extracts show the **totals** of the Analysed Cash Book (Analysed Receipts and Payments Book) in euros, for the month ending 31.5.05.

**Analysed Cash Book (Debit Side)**

| Date | Details | Bank | Shops | Bars | Homes | Other |
|---|---|---|---|---|---|---|
| 31.5.05 | Total | 6,500 | 3,500 | 500 | 1,500 | 1,000 |

**Analysed Cash Book (Credit Side)**

| Date | Details | Bank | Phone | Petrol | Wages | Postage |
|---|---|---|---|---|---|---|
| 31.5.05 | Total | 4,800 | 800 | 800 | 2,900 | 300 |

As their accountant you are asked to prepare a *Receipts and Payments Account* for the month of May 2005.

4. Travel Ltd sells holidays within Ireland. On 1 June 2006, the firm has a bank overdraft of €3,500. The following extracts show the totals of the Analysed Cash Book, in euros, for the month ending 30.6.06.

**Analysed Cash Book (Debit Side)**

| Date | Details | Bank | Leinster | Munster | Ulster | Connaught |
|---|---|---|---|---|---|---|
| 30.6.06 | Total | 17,400 | 8,000 | 4,500 | 2,800 | 2,100 |

**Analysed Cash Book (Credit Side)**

| Date | Details | Bank | Wages | Rent | Phone | Postage |
|---|---|---|---|---|---|---|
| 30.6.06 | Total | 12,800 | 6,300 | 2,500 | 3,500 | 500 |

As their accountant you are asked to prepare a *Receipts and Payments Account* for the month of June 2006.

5. Write up the *Analysed Cash Book* (Analysed Receipts and Payments Book) of Fitt Ltd, a health club, for the month of October 2006 from the following information.

   Use the following money column headings:

   **Debit (Receipts) side:** Bank, Gym, Pool, Snooker
   **Credit (Payments) side:** Bank, Wages, Light and Heat, Repairs, Other

| | | | € |
|---|---|---|---|
| *1.10.06* | *Cash in Bank* | | *1,900* |
| *2.10.06* | *Gym receipts* | *Receipt No. 101* | *1,500* |
| *3.10.06* | *Pool receipts* | *Receipt No. 102* | *1,300* |
| *3.10.06* | *Paid wages* | *Cheque No. 15* | *550* |
| *5.10.06* | *Snooker receipts* | *Receipt No. 103* | *1,000* |

| | | | |
|---|---|---|---|
| *5.10.06* | *Paid wages* | *Cheque No. 16* | *340* |
| *6.10.06* | *Paid ESB bill* | *Cheque No. 17* | *300* |
| *9.10.06* | *Purchased new equipment* | *Cheque No. 18* | *2,000* |
| *12.10.06* | *Paid for heating oil* | *Cheque No. 19* | *560* |
| *14.10.06* | *Paid wages* | *Cheque No. 20* | *500* |
| *18.10.06* | *Paid insurance* | *Cheque No. 21* | *850* |
| *20.10.06* | *Paid wages* | *Cheque No. 22* | *800* |
| *21.10.06* | *Gym receipts* | *Receipt No. 104* | *2,050* |
| *22.10.06* | *Pool receipts* | *Receipt No. 105* | *1,850* |
| *23.10.06* | *Repairs to pool* | *Cheque No. 23* | *500* |
| *24.10.06* | *Repairs to snooker table* | *Cheque No. 24* | *150* |
| *25.10.06* | *Paid advertising* | *Cheque No. 25* | *400* |
| *28.10.06* | *Receipts from snooker* | *Receipt No. 106* | *1,700* |
| *31.10.06* | *Paid wages* | *Cheque No. 26* | *500* |

## 4.2 OPERATING STATEMENT

The operating statement of a service firm is similar to the Trading, Profit and Loss Account of a trading firm with the following exceptions.

*Figure 4.2*

| **Trading, Profit and Loss Account** | **Operating Statement** |
|---|---|
| Sales | Customer Receipts |
| Purchases | These generally do not exist in Service Firm Accounts as they do not buy stock for resale |
| Opening and Closing Stocks | |

It contains the following information:

- Income received during the year. (e.g. Customer Receipts)
- Income due at the end of the year is added. (e.g. Customer Receipts due)
- Expenses paid during the year. (e.g. Insurance)
- Expenses due at the end of the year are added. (e.g. Insurance due)
- Expenses prepaid at the end of the year are subtracted. (e.g. Insurance prepaid)
- A profit or loss is then calculated.

***Example***

Barford Kennels Ltd owns a dog and cat hotel. They have supplied you with the following information and ask you to prepare the Operating Statement for the year ended 31 December 1999.

| Income for the year | IR£ | Expenditure for the year | IR£ |
|---|---|---|---|
| Cat Boarding | 18,000 | Wages | 7,500 |
| Dog Boarding | 12,000 | Feed | 5,500 |
| | | Electricity | 1,750 |
| | | Insurance | 1,250 |
| | | Vet Fees | 350 |
| | | Repairs | 1,850 |
| | | Rent | 1,350 |

| Assets | IR£ | Liabilities | IR£ |
|---|---|---|---|
| Land | 100,000 | Loan | 50,000 |
| Buildings | 44,000 | Creditors | 500 |
| Debtors | 750 | Capital | 90,000 |
| Bank | 5,500 | | |
| Cash | 700 | | |

You are given the following additional information as at 31 December 1999:

*(i) Wages due* *IR£400*
*(ii) Insurance prepaid* *IR£250*
*(iii) The buildings are to be depreciated by 2%*

The following reminders should prove useful before attempting the solution.

*Income Due*

- **Add** the amount due to the amount already received in the **Income** section of the **Operating Statement**
- Record the amount due as a **Current Asset** in the **Balance Sheet**

*Income Prepaid*

- **Deduct** the amount prepaid from the amount already received in the **Income** section of the **Operating Statement**
- Record the amount prepaid as a **Current Liability** in the **Balance Sheet**

*Expenses Due (Accrued Expenses)*

- **Add** the amount due to the amount already paid in the **Expenditure** section of the **Operating Statement**
- Record the amount due as a **Current Liability** in the **Balance Sheet**

*Expenses Prepaid*

- **Deduct** the amount prepaid from the amount already paid in the **Expenditure** section of the **Operating Statement**
- Record the amount prepaid as a **Current Asset** in the **Balance Sheet**

*SOLUTION*

| Operating Statement of Barford Kennels Ltd for the year ended 31 December 1999 | | | |
|---|---|---|---|
| **Income** | **IR£** | **IR£** | **IR£** |
| Cat Boarding | | 18,000 | |
| Dog Boarding | | 12,000 | |
| **Total Income** | | | 30,000 |
| | | | |
| **Less Expenditure** | | | |
| Wages | 7,500 | | |
| Add Wages Due | 400 | 7,900 | |
| Feed | | 5,500 | |
| Electricity | | 1,750 | |
| Insurance | 1,250 | | |
| Less Insurance Prepaid | 250 | 1,000 | |
| Vet Fees | | 350 | |
| Repairs | | 1,850 | |
| Rent | | 1,350 | |
| Depreciation Buildings | | 880 | |
| **Total Expenditure** | | | 20,580 |
| | | | |
| **Net Profit** | | | 9,420 |

## Practice Questions

1. New Pin Ltd operates an ironing and cleaning service for householders. From the information provided in the Trial Balance on 31 December 2000 you are required to prepare:

   An *Operating Statement* (Trading, Profit and Loss Account) for the year ended 31.12.00.

| Trial Balance as at 31 December 2000 | | |
|---|---|---|
| | **DR IR£** | **CR IR£** |
| Motor Vehicles | 20,000 | |
| Equipment | 18,000 | |
| Debtors | 1,500 | |
| Sales Ironing | | 2,000 |
| Cleaning | | 3,500 |
| Shampooing | | 2,300 |
| Wages | 1,500 | |
| Materials | 1,500 | |
| Telephone | 250 | |

| Trial Balance as at 31 December 2000 *contd.* | | |
|---|---|---|
| | DR IR£ | CR IR£ |
| Insurance | 1,500 | |
| Repairs to equipment | 220 | |
| Petrol | 130 | |
| Bank | 3,400 | |
| Creditors | | 200 |
| Loan | | 10,000 |
| Capital | | 30,000 |
| | 48,000 | 48,000 |

2. Sherlock Solicitors, a service firm, are based in Dublin. They provided the following information and have asked you to prepare the *Operating Statement* (Trading, Profit and Loss Account) for the year ended 31 December 2003.

| Income for the year | € | Expenditure for the year | € |
|---|---|---|---|
| Court fees | 12,300 | Wages | 7,750 |
| House sales | 8,040 | Light and Heat | 2,570 |
| Wills | 9,900 | Stationery | 920 |
| | | Insurance | 2,220 |
| | | Telephone | 685 |
| | | Rent | 3,000 |
| | | Repairs | 1,240 |
| | | Rates | 1,300 |
| | | Loan Interest | 1,500 |

| Assets | € | Liabilities | € |
|---|---|---|---|
| Buildings | 60,000 | Bank Overdraft | 2,000 |
| Equipment | 13,000 | Creditors | 3,350 |
| Debtors | 1,405 | Capital | 50,000 |
| | | Loan | 10,000 |

You are given the following additional information as at 31 Dec. 2003:

*(i) Court fees due €700*
*(ii) Rates due €200*
*(iii) Insurance prepaid €220*
*(iv) The equipment is to be depreciated by 10%*

3. Safe Systems Ltd operate an alarm monitoring service for both residential and commercial properties. From the information provided in the Trial Balance on 31 December 2004 you are required to prepare:

An *Operating Statement* (Trading, Profit and Loss Account) for the year ended 31.12.04

| Trial Balance as at 31 December 2004 | | |
|---|---|---|
| | DR € | CR € |
| Motor Vehicles | 20,000 | |
| Equipment | 28,000 | |
| Debtors | 1,820 | |
| Fees Residential | | 12,000 |
| Commercial | | 13,500 |
| Wages | 9,950 | |
| Light and Heat | 1,880 | |
| Telephone | 750 | |
| Insurance | 2,200 | |
| Repairs to equipment | 1,500 | |
| Rates | 1,200 | |
| Cash at Bank | 3,400 | |
| Creditors | | 200 |
| Loan | | 10,000 |
| Ordinary Share Capital | | 35,000 |
| | 70,700 | 70,700 |

The following additional information is provided at the year-end:

*(i) Light and heat paid in advance €380*
*(ii) Rates due €300*
*(iii) Depreciate: Motor Vehicles by 20%*
*Equipment by 10%*

## 4.3 BALANCE SHEET

- ▶ Records the assets and liabilities of the service firm
- ▶ Similar format to the Balance Sheet of a firm
- ▶ Adjustments (accruals and prepayments) are included
- ▶ A net profit or net loss is added to or subtracted from the capital

### Comprehensive Example

Barford Kennels Ltd owns a dog and cat hotel. They have supplied you with the following information and ask you to prepare the following:

(a) Operating Statement for the year ended 31 December 1999
(b) Balance Sheet as at 31 December 1999

| Income for the year | IR£ | Expenditure for the year | IR£ |
|---|---|---|---|
| Cat Boarding | 18,000 | Wages | 7,500 |
| Dog Boarding | 12,000 | Feed | 5,500 |
| | | Electricity | 1,750 |
| | | Insurance | 1,250 |
| | | Vet Fees | 350 |
| | | Repairs | 1,850 |
| | | Rent | 1,350 |

| Assets | IR£ | Liabilities | IR£ |
|---|---|---|---|
| Land | 100,000 | Loan | 50,000 |
| Buildings | 44,000 | Creditors | 500 |
| Debtors | 750 | Capital | 90,000 |
| Bank | 5,500 | | |
| Cash | 700 | | |

You are given the following additional information as at 31 December 1999:

*(i) Wages due IR£400*
*(ii) Insurance prepaid IR£250*
*(iii) The buildings are to be depreciated by 2%*

*SOLUTION*

| Operating Statement of Barford Kennels Ltd for the year ended 31 December 1999 | | | |
|---|---|---|---|
| **Income** | **IR£** | **IR£** | **IR£** |
| Cat Boarding | | 18,000 | |
| Dog Boarding | | 12,000 | |
| **Total Income** | | | 30,000 |
| | | | |
| **Less Expenditure** | | | |
| Wages | 7,500 | | |
| Add Wages Due | 400 | 7,900 | |
| Feed | | 5,500 | |
| Electricity | | 1,750 | |
| Insurance | 1,250 | | |
| Less Insurance Prepaid | 250 | 1,000 | |
| Vet Fees | | 350 | |
| Repairs | | 1,850 | |
| Rent | | 1,350 | |
| Depreciation Buildings | | 880 | |
| **Total Expenditure** | | | 20,580 |
| | | | |
| **Net Profit** | | | 9,420 |

| Balance Sheet of Barford Kennels Ltd as at 31 December 1999 | | | |
|---|---|---|---|
| | IR£ | IR£ | IR£ |
| **Fixed Assets** | **Cost** | **Deprec** | **NBV** |
| Land | 100,000 | | 100,000 |
| Buildings | 44,000 | 880 | 43,120 |
| | 144,000 | 880 | 143,120 |
| **Current Assets** | | | |
| Debtors | | 750 | |
| Bank | | 5,500 | |
| Cash | | 700 | |
| Insurance Prepaid | | 250 | |
| | | 7,200 | |
| **Less Current Liabilities** | | | |
| Creditors | 500 | | |
| Wages due | 400 | 900 | |
| Working capital | | | 6,300 |
| **Total Net Assets** | | | 149,420 |
| **Financed By:** | | | |
| Capital | | | 90,000 |
| Add Net Profit | | | 9,420 |
| | | | 99,420 |
| **Long Term Liabilities** | | | |
| Loan | | | 50,000 |
| **Capital Employed** | | | 149,420 |

## 4.4 COMBINATION QUESTIONS

1. New Pin Ltd operates an ironing and cleaning service for householders. From the information provided in the Trial Balance on 31 December 2000 you are required to prepare:

   (a) An *Operating Statement* (Trading, Profit and Loss Account) for the year ended 31.12.00

   (b) A *Balance Sheet* as at 31.12.00

| Trial Balance as at 31 December 2000 | | |
|---|---|---|
| | DR IR£ | CR IR£ |
| Motor Vehicles | 20,000 | |
| Equipment | 18,000 | |
| Debtors | 1,500 | |
| Sales Ironing | | 2,000 |
| Cleaning | | 3,500 |
| Shampooing | | 2,300 |
| Wages | 1,500 | |
| Materials | 1,500 | |
| Telephone | 250 | |
| Insurance | 1,500 | |
| Repairs to equipment | 220 | |
| Petrol | 130 | |
| Bank | 3,400 | |
| Creditors | | 200 |
| Loan | | 10,000 |
| Capital | | 30,000 |
| | 48,000 | 48,000 |

2. Safe Systems Ltd operate an alarm monitoring service for both residential and commercial properties. From the information provided in the Trial Balance on 31 December 2004 you are required to prepare:

   (a) An *Operating Statement* (Trading, Profit and Loss Account) for the year ended 31.12.04

   (b) A *Balance Sheet* as at 31.12.04

| Trial Balance as at 31 December 2004 | | |
|---|---|---|
| | DR € | CR € |
| Motor Vehicles | 20,000 | |
| Equipment | 28,000 | |
| Debtors | 1,820 | |
| Fees Residential | | 12,000 |
| Commercial | | 13,500 |
| Wages | 9,950 | |
| Light and Heat | 1,880 | |
| Telephone | 750 | |
| Insurance | 2,200 | |
| Repairs to equipment | 1,500 | |
| Rates | 1,200 | |
| Cash at Bank | 3,400 | |

| **Trial Balance as at 31 December 2004 *contd.*** | | |
|---|---|---|
| | **DR €** | **CR €** |
| Creditors | | 200 |
| Loan | | 10,000 |
| Ordinary Share Capital | | 35,000 |
| | 70,700 | 70,700 |

The following additional information is provided at the year-end:

*(i) Light and Heat paid in advance €380*
*(ii) Rates due €300*
*(iii) Depreciate: Motor Vehicles by 20%*
*Equipment by 10%*

3. Mr. McCavity runs a dental surgery in his local town and has kept double-entry accounts. The following Trial Balance was extracted on 31.12.05.

You are required to prepare:

(a) An *Operating Statement* (Trading, Profit and Loss Account) for the year ended 31.12.05
(b) A *Balance Sheet* as at 31.12.05

The following additional adjustments are provided at the year-end:

*(i) Light and Heat in arrears €225*
*(ii) Insurance due €100*
*(iii) Depreciate the equipment by 5%*

| **Trial Balance as at 31 December 2005** | | | |
|---|---|---|---|
| | | **DR €** | **CR €** |
| Premises | | 100,000 | |
| Equipment | | 30,000 | |
| Debtors | | 4,500 | |
| Fees | Dental Work | | 28,250 |
| | Toothbrushes | | 4,500 |
| | Toothpaste | | 2,550 |
| Rent | | 5,500 | |
| Rates | | 2,500 | |
| Telephone | | 1,200 | |
| Insurance | | 1,900 | |
| Light and Heat | | 775 | |
| Dental supplies | | 2,525 | |

| Trial Balance as at 31 December 2005 *contd.* | | |
|---|---|---|
| | DR € | CR € |
| Secretary's wages | 9,950 | |
| Creditors | | 3,550 |
| Loan | | 20,000 |
| Ordinary Share Capital | | 100,000 |
| | 158,850 | 158,850 |

4. LCM Ltd, a boat-hire firm, hires boats on lakes in Counties Leitrim, Cavan and Monaghan. From the information provided in the Trial Balance on 31 December 2005 you are required to prepare:

   (a) An *Operating Statement* (Trading, Profit and Loss Account) for the year ended 31.12.05

   (b) A *Balance Sheet* as at 31.12.05

| Trial Balance as at 31 December 2005 | | |
|---|---|---|
| | DR € | CR € |
| Boats | 35,000 | |
| Equipment | 18,000 | |
| Bank Overdraft | | 1,000 |
| Rental Leitrim | | 10,000 |
| Cavan | | 10,800 |
| Monaghan | | 11,500 |
| Wages | 12,770 | |
| Boat repairs | 4,900 | |
| Telephone | 230 | |
| Insurance | 3,600 | |
| Repairs to equipment | 1,600 | |
| Fishing permits | 2,000 | |
| Advertising | 2,400 | |
| Creditors | | 2,200 |
| Term Loan | | 10,000 |
| Ordinary Share Capital | | 35,000 |
| | 80,500 | 80,500 |

The following additional information is provided at the year-end:

*(i) Insurance paid in advance* *€600*

*(ii) Advertising due* *€200*

*(iii) Depreciate: Boats by 10%*

*Equipment by 10%*

# CHAPTER 5
# FARM ACCOUNTS

## Introduction

In the Irish economy agriculture is one of the most important industries. Farming is a business, therefore it is essential that proper records and accounts are kept for many reasons. These are summarised below:

- ▶ To calculate the profit or loss of the farm for a particular period
- ▶ To calculate which farm activities are most profitable
- ▶ To analyse and compare with previous figures in order to make sound and efficient decisions (e.g. the feasibility of future expansion)
- ▶ To present information to the Government for taxation purposes or for the application of a government/EU grant
- ▶ To calculate how much the farm is worth

*The Accounts*

The accounts maintained by a farmer are similar to those kept by a club, as shown below:

- ▶ Analysed Cash Book (to record daily receipts and payments)
- ▶ Income and Expenditure Account (to calculate profit or loss)
- ▶ Balance Sheet (a statement of assets, liabilities and capital)

## 5.1 ANALYSED CASH BOOK

The accounting treatment of this account is similar to that of an analysed receipts and payments account of a club.

- ▶ Records the daily receipts and payments of the farmer
- ▶ Analysed in the same manner as the analysed cash book of a normal business
- ▶ Monies received are entered on the DEBIT side
- ▶ Monies paid are entered on the CREDIT side

*Example*

Dinny and Teasie own a farm in Wicklow and have a balance of IR£3,500 in the bank on 1 May, 1997. They ask you to help them to write up their *Analysed Cash Book* (Analysed Receipts and Payments Account) for the month of May, 1997 from the data below:

Use the following money column headings:

**Debit (Receipts) side:** Bank, Sheep, Cattle, Grants, Other
**Credit (Payments) side:** Bank, Feed, Fertiliser, Cattle, Vet, Expenses, Other

| | | | *IR£* |
|---|---|---|---|
| *2.5.97* | *Paid the vet* | *Cheque No. 11* | *130* |
| *5.5.97* | *Sale of sheep* | *Receipt No. 2* | *1,600* |
| *8.5.97* | *Purchased calves* | *Cheque No. 12* | *1,500* |
| *12.5.97* | *Received EU grant* | | *2,000* |
| *13.5.97* | *Purchased fertiliser* | *Cheque No. 13* | *400* |
| *16.5.97* | *Purchased feed* | *Cheque No. 14* | *200* |
| *19.5.97* | *Paid ESB* | *Cheque No. 15* | *165* |
| *21.5.97* | *Sold cattle* | *Receipt No. 3* | *3,000* |
| *24.5.97* | *Paid insurance* | *Cheque No. 16* | *460* |
| *27.5.97* | *Received a Loan* | | *12,000* |
| *28.5.97* | *Paid contractor* | *Cheque No. 17* | *18,500* |
| *30.5.97* | *Purchased tractor* | *Cheque No. 18* | *5,700* |
| *31.5.97* | *Sold cattle* | *Receipt No. 4* | *6,900* |
| *31.5.97* | *Sale of vegetables* | *Receipt No. 5* | *145* |

(Junior Certificate Higher Level 1997, Paper II, Q6(b))

*SOLUTION*

| **Debit side (Receipts)** | | | | | | | |
|---|---|---|---|---|---|---|---|
| **Date** | **Details** | **Receipt No.** | **Bank** | **Sheep** | **Cattle** | **Grants** | **Other** |
| 1.5.97 | Balance b/d | | 3,500 | | | | |
| 5.5.97 | Sales | 2 | 1,600 | 1,600 | | | |
| 12.5.97 | EU grant | | 2,000 | | | 2,000 | |
| 21.5.97 | Sales | 3 | 3,000 | | 3,000 | | |
| 27.5.97 | Loan | | 12,000 | | | | 12,000 |
| 31.5.97 | Sales | 4 | 6,900 | | 6,900 | | |
| 31.5.97 | Sales | 5 | 145 | | | | 145 |
| | | | 29,145 | 1,600 | 9,900 | 2,000 | 12,145 |
| 1.6.97 | Balance b/d | | 2,090 | | | | |

| Credit side (Payments) | | | | | | | | |
|---|---|---|---|---|---|---|---|---|
| **Date** | **Details** | **Chq No.** | **Bank** | **Feed** | **Fertiliser** | **Cattle** | **Vet** | **Expenses** |
| 2.5.97 | Vet bill | 11 | 130 | | | | 130 | |
| 8.5.97 | Calves | 12 | 1,500 | | | 1,500 | | |
| 13.5.97 | Fertiliser | 13 | 400 | | 400 | | | |
| 16.5.97 | Feed | 14 | 200 | 200 | | | | |
| 19.5.97 | ESB | 15 | 165 | | | | | 165 |
| 24.5.97 | Insurance | 16 | 460 | | | | | 460 |
| 28.5.97 | Contractor | 17 | 18,500 | | | | | 18,500 |
| 30.5.97 | Tractor | 18 | 5,700 | | | | | 5,700 |
| 31.5.97 | Balance c/d | | 2,090 | | | | | |
| | | | 29,145 | 200 | 400 | 1,500 | 130 | 24,825 |

**Note** *The bank column is the only column that is actually balanced*
*The analysis columns are totalled independently of each other*
*Be careful not to forget about the opening bank balance*
*For more detailed instruction, refer back to Club Accounts*

## Practice Questions

1. Noel Lucas owns a farm in Louth and has a balance of IR£500 in the bank on 1 July 2001. He asks you to write up the *Analysed Cash Book* (Analysed Receipts and Payments Account) for the month of July 2001 from the data below.

   Use the following money column headings:

   **Debit (Receipts) side:** Bank, Grain, Cattle, Poultry, Grants
   **Credit (Payments) side:** Bank, Feed, Fertiliser, Cattle, Expenses, Other

| | | | *IR£* |
|---|---|---|---|
| *6.7.01* | *Sold grain* | *Receipt No. 12* | *10,600* |
| *9.7.01* | *Purchased cattle* | *Cheque No. 112* | *2,500* |
| *13.7.01* | *Received EU grant* | | *1,000* |
| *14.7.01* | *Purchased fertiliser* | *Cheque No. 113* | *2,400* |
| *17.7.01* | *Purchased feed* | *Cheque No. 114* | *1,200* |
| *18.7.01* | *Bought diesel oil* | *Cheque No. 115* | *1,165* |
| *21.7.01* | *Sold cattle* | *Receipt No. 13* | *2,000* |
| *25.7.01* | *Paid tractor insurance* | *Cheque No. 116* | *700* |
| *27.7.01* | *Sold grain* | *Receipt No. 14* | *11,000* |
| *29.7.01* | *Paid contractor* | *Cheque No. 117* | *18,500* |
| *30.7.01* | *Purchased machinery* | *Cheque No. 118* | *1,500* |
| *31.7.01* | *Sold cattle* | *Receipt No. 15* | *6,900* |
| *31.7.01* | *Sale of eggs* | *Receipt No. 16* | *145* |

2. Janet James owns an arable farm in Tipperary. She lodged €3,000 in the bank on 1 October 2002. She asks you to write up the *Analysed Cash Book* (Analysed Receipts and Payments Account) for the month of October 2002 from the data below.

   Use the following money column headings:

   **Debit (Receipts) side:** Bank, Wheat, Barley, Oats, Grants
   **Credit (Payments) side:** Bank, Fertiliser, Seed, Expenses, Other

| | | | € |
|---|---|---|---|
| *4.10.02* | *Purchased grain seed* | *Cheque No. 50* | *7,500* |
| *6.10.02* | *Purchased fertiliser* | *Cheque No. 51* | *2,500* |
| *11.10.02* | *Received EU grant* | | *4,000* |
| *13.10.02* | *Purchased fertiliser* | *Cheque No. 52* | *4,500* |
| *16.10.02* | *Purchased grain seed* | *Cheque No. 53* | *2,900* |
| *18.10.02* | *Paid wages* | *Cheque No. 54* | *2,850* |
| *22.10.02* | *Sold grain* | *Receipt No. 33* | |
| | *Barley* | | *6,500* |
| | *Wheat* | | *4,450* |
| | *Oats* | | *4,600* |
| *24.10.02* | *Paid insurance* | *Cheque No. 55* | *1,850* |
| *25.10.02* | *Sold grain* | *Receipt No. 34* | |
| | *Barley* | | *6,950* |
| | *Wheat* | | *4,250* |
| | *Oats* | | *3,330* |
| *28.10.02* | *Purchased combine harvester* | *Cheque No. 56* | *19,950* |
| *30.10.02* | *Paid wages* | *Cheque No. 57* | *2,500* |
| *31.10.02* | *Sold grain* | *Receipt No. 35* | |
| | *Barley* | | *3,500* |
| | *Wheat* | | *3,220* |
| | *Oats* | | *3,680* |

3. Brian Sherry farms a mixed farm in Galway. His bank account shows there is an overdraft of €4,500 on 1 November 2004. He asks you to write up the *Analysed Cash Book* (Analysed Receipts and Payments Account) for the month of November 2004 from the data below.

   Use the following money column headings:

   **Debit (Receipts) side:** Bank, Sheep, Pigs, Dairy, Grants
   **Credit (Payments) side:** Bank, Vet, Feed, Expenses, Other

| | | | € |
|---|---|---|---|
| *3.11.04* | *Paid veterinary fees* | *Cheque No. 10* | *500* |
| *6.11.04* | *Purchased animal foodstuffs* | *Cheque No. 11* | *1,880* |
| *12.11.04* | *EU financial assistance* | | *5,500* |
| *14.11.04* | *Purchased new tractor* | *Cheque No. 12* | *5,400* |

| | | | |
|---|---|---|---|
| *17.11.04* | *Purchased animal foodstuffs* | *Cheque No. 13* | *870* |
| *19.11.04* | *Paid insurance* | *Cheque No. 14* | *850* |
| *20.11.04* | *Sold sheep and lambs* | *Receipt No. 44* | *3,200* |
| *24.11.04* | *Sold pigs* | *Receipt No. 45* | *2,050* |
| *26.11.04* | *Received creamery cheque* | *Receipt No. 46* | *4,440* |
| *28.11.04* | *Paid light and heat* | *Cheque No. 15* | *950* |
| *29.11.04* | *Paid wages* | *Cheque No. 16* | *490* |
| *30.11.04* | *Sold milk to his neighbours* | *Receipt No. 47* | *35* |

4. Maureen Wilson has a farm in Co. Carlow. On 1 January 2005, she has €885 in the bank. The following extracts show the **totals** of the Analysed Cash Book (Analysed Receipts and Payments Account) in euros, for the month ending 31.1.05.

**Analysed Cash Book (Debit Side)**

| Date | Details | Bank | Cattle | Sheep | Poultry | Grants |
|---|---|---|---|---|---|---|
| 31.01.05 | Total | 5,500 | 2,500 | 1,500 | 500 | 1,000 |

**Analysed Cash Book (Credit Side)**

| Date | Details | Bank | Feed | Vet | Exps. | Land |
|---|---|---|---|---|---|---|
| 31.01.05 | Total | 3,335 | 455 | 180 | 700 | 2,000 |

As her accountant she asks you to prepare a *Receipts and Payments Account* for the month of January 2005.

5. Peter Thompson owns a farm in Co. Mayo. On 1 May 2006, his bank account shows an overdraft of €1,235. The following extracts show the **totals** of the Analysed Cash Book (Analysed Receipts and Payments Account) in euros, for the month ending 31.5.06.

**Analysed Cash Book (Debit Side)**

| Date | Details | Bank | Sheep | Lambs | Wool | Grants |
|---|---|---|---|---|---|---|
| 31.05.06 | Total | 2,225 | 1,110 | 500 | 390 | 225 |

**Analysed Cash Book (Credit Side)**

| Date | Details | Bank | Feed | Vet | Rent | ESB |
|---|---|---|---|---|---|---|
| 31.05.06 | Total | 2,505 | 298 | 88 | 1,700 | 419 |

As her accountant she asks you to prepare a *Receipts and Payments Account* for the month of May 2006.

## 5.2 INCOME AND EXPENDITURE ACCOUNT

- Records the income and expenditure of the farm
- Prepared in an easier format than the Profit and Loss account of a firm
- Adjustments are treated in the same manner as those in the final accounts of a firm
- If income is greater than expenditure, the excess is known as a profit
- If expenditure is greater than income, the difference is known as a loss

**Reminder** *The Income and Expenditure Account does not take into account the following:*

- *Opening and closing cash/bank balances.*
- *The purchase and/or sale of fixed assets.*

*Example*

Tom and Tina Murphy keep farm accounts. They have supplied you with the following annual records and ask you to prepare an *Income and Expenditure Account* for the year ended 31 December 1999.

| **Income for the year ended 31.12.99** | **IR£** |
|---|---|
| Livestock | 8,880 |
| Sheep | 1,550 |
| Pork | 1,000 |
| Poultry | 450 |

| **Expenses for the year ended 31.12.99** | **IR£** |
|---|---|
| Wages | 2,000 |
| Rent | 1,800 |
| Insurance | 300 |
| Feed | 1,150 |
| Vet fees | 320 |
| Fertilisers | 655 |
| Repairs | 480 |
| Hire of machinery | 2,050 |

*Solution*

| **Income and Expenditure Account of Tom and Tina Murphy for the year ended 31 December 1999** | | | |
|---|---|---|---|
| **Income** | **IR£** | **IR£** | **IR£** |
| Livestock | | 8,880 | |
| Sheep | | 1,550 | |
| Pork | | 1,000 | |
| Poultry | | 450 | |
| **Total Income** | | | 11,880 |

| Income and Expenditure Account of Tom and Tina Murphy for the year ended 31 December 1999 *contd.* | | | |
|---|---|---|---|
| | **IR£** | **IR£** | **IR£** |
| **Less Expenditure** | | | |
| Wages | | 2,000 | |
| Rent | | 1,800 | |
| Insurance | | 300 | |
| Feed | | 1,150 | |
| Vet fees | | 320 | |
| Fertilisers | | 655 | |
| Repairs | | 480 | |
| Hire of machinery | | 2,050 | |
| **Total Expenditure** | | | 8,755 |
| **Farm Profit** | | | 3,125 |

## Practice Questions

1. David Davidson, a farmer, keeps farm accounts. From the following information prepare a Statement of *Income and Expenditure* for the year ended 31 December 2001.

| **Income for the year ended 31.12.01** | **IR£** |
|---|---|
| Cattle | 14,760 |
| Sheep and wool | 11,090 |
| Dairy products | 1,230 |
| Poultry | 2,450 |
| Pigs | 2,000 |

| **Expenses for the year ended 31.12.01** | **IR£** |
|---|---|
| Rent | 8,800 |
| Wages | 1,800 |
| Insurance | 2,330 |
| Feed | 3,890 |
| Vet fees | 390 |
| Fertilisers | 1,585 |
| Repairs | 480 |
| Contractor | 7,770 |

2. Moira Molloy keeps farm accounts and at the end of each financial year she prepares a *Statement of Income and Expenditure.* Prepare this statement from the following information for the year ended 31 July 2003.

| **Income for the year ended 31.07.03** | **€** |
| --- | ---: |
| Cattle | 12,450 |
| Sheep and wool | 8,770 |
| Milk | 4,320 |
| Poultry | 985 |
| Pigs | 1,445 |
| Miscellaneous current income | 3,085 |

| **Expenses for the year ended 31.07.03** | **€** |
| --- | ---: |
| Rent of conacre | 13,355 |
| Animal foodstuffs | 4,400 |
| Rates | 1,555 |
| Wages | 2,980 |
| Vet fees | 85 |
| Fertilisers | 505 |
| Light and Heat | 315 |
| Hire of equipment and machinery | 2,205 |

3. Mark Conlon runs a mixed farm and keeps accounts. At the end of each financial year he prepares a *Statement of Income and Expenditure.* He asks you to prepare this statement from the following information for the year ended 31 May 2005.

| **Income for the year ended 31.05.05** | **€** |
| --- | ---: |
| Livestock | 10,480 |
| Sheep and wool | 18,770 |
| Milk | 14,320 |
| Fruit | 508 |
| Vegetables | 112 |
| Poultry | 985 |
| EU financial assistance | 4,445 |
| Rent receivable | 775 |

| **Expenses for the year ended 31.05.05** | **€** |
| --- | ---: |
| Rent of conacre | 11,145 |
| Animal foodstuffs | 17,400 |
| Rates | 1,005 |
| Wages | 5,770 |
| Vet fees | 2,785 |
| Fertilisers | 1,335 |
| Light and Heat | 888 |
| Hire of equipment and machinery | 4,450 |
| Seeds | 332 |
| Telephone | 449 |
| Contractor | 2,500 |

## Income and Expenditure Account with Adjustments

For detail regarding the preparation of an income and expenditure account including adjustments refer back to chapter 3 — CLUB ACCOUNTS.

The following reminders should prove useful before attempting the solution:

### *Income Due*

- ▶ **Add** the amount due to the amount already received in the **Income** section of the **Income and Expenditure Account**
- ▶ Record the amount due as a **Current Asset** in the **Balance Sheet**

### *Income Prepaid*

- ▶ **Deduct** the amount prepaid from the amount already received in the **Income** section of the **Income and Expenditure Account**
- ▶ Record the amount prepaid as a **Current Liability** in the **Balance Sheet**

### *Expenses Due (Accrued Expenses)*

- ▶ **Add** the amount due to the amount already paid in the **Expenditure** section of the **Income and Expenditure Account**
- ▶ Record the amount due as a **Current Liability** in the **Balance Sheet**

### *Expenses Prepaid*

- ▶ **Deduct** the amount prepaid from the amount already paid in the **Expenditure** section of the **Income and Expenditure Account**
- ▶ Record the amount prepaid as a **Current Asset** in the **Balance Sheet**

### *Example*

Using the previous example, Tom and Tina Murphy, prepare the *Income and Expenditure Account* for the year ended 31 December 1999 taking into account the following:

*(i) Wages due* *IR£200*
*(ii) Insurance prepaid* *IR£100*

*SOLUTION*

| Income and Expenditure Account of Tom and Tina Murphy for the year ended 31 December 1999 | | | |
|---|---|---|---|
| **Income** | **IR£** | **IR£** | **IR£** |
| Livestock | | 8,880 | |
| Sheep | | 1,550 | |
| Pork | | 1,000 | |
| Poultry | | 450 | |
| **Total Income** | | | 11,880 |
| **Less Expenditure** | | | |
| Wages | 2,000 | | |
| Add Wages Due | 200 | 2,200 | |
| Rent | | 1,800 | |
| Insurance | 300 | | |
| Less Insurance Prepaid | 100 | 200 | |
| Feed | | 1,150 | |
| Vet fees | | 320 | |
| Fertilisers | | 655 | |
| Repairs | | 480 | |
| Hire of machinery | | 2,050 | |
| **Total Expenditure** | | | 8,855 |
| **Farm Profit** | | | 3,025 |

## Practice Questions

1. David Davidson, a farmer, keeps farm accounts. From the following information prepare a *Statement of Income and Expenditure* for the year ended 31 December 2001.

| **Income for the year ended 31.12.01** | **IR£** |
|---|---|
| Cattle | 14,760 |
| Sheep and wool | 11,090 |
| Dairy products | 1,230 |
| Poultry | 2,450 |
| Pigs | 2,000 |

| **Expenses for the year ended 31.12.01** | **IR£** |
|---|---|
| Rent | 8,800 |
| Wages | 1,800 |
| Insurance | 2,330 |

| | |
|---|---|
| Feed | 3,890 |
| Vet fees | 390 |
| Fertilisers | 1,585 |
| Repairs | 480 |
| Contractor | 7,770 |

You are given the following additional information as at 31 Dec 2001:

*(i) Rent prepaid IR£800*
*(ii) Wages due IR£200*

2. Moira Molloy keeps farm accounts and at the end of each financial year she prepares a *Statement of Income and Expenditure.* Prepare this statement from the following information for the year ended 31 July 2003.

| **Income for the year ended 31.07.03** | **€** |
|---|---|
| Cattle | 12,450 |
| Sheep and wool | 8,770 |
| Milk | 4,320 |
| Poultry | 985 |
| Pigs | 1,445 |
| Miscellaneous current income | 3,085 |
| **Expenses for the year ended 31.07.03** | **€** |
| Rent of conacre | 13,355 |
| Animal foodstuffs | 4,400 |
| Rates | 1,555 |
| Wages | 2,980 |
| Vet fees | 85 |
| Fertilisers | 505 |
| Light and heat | 315 |
| Hire of equipment and machinery | 2,205 |

You are given the following additional information as at 31 July 2003:

*(i) Rent prepaid €755*
*(ii) Rates prepaid €145*
*(iii) Wages due €220*
*(iv) Light and heat due €185*

3. Mark Conlon runs a mixed farm and keeps accounts. At the end of each financial year he prepares a *Statement of Income and Expenditure.* He asks you to prepare this statement from the following information for the year ended 31 May 2005.

| **Income for the year ended 31.05.05** | **€** |
|---|---|
| Livestock | 10,480 |
| Sheep and wool | 18,770 |
| Milk | 14,320 |
| Fruit | 508 |
| Vegetables | 112 |
| Poultry | 985 |
| EU financial assistance | 4,445 |
| Rent receivable | 775 |

| **Expenses for the year ended 31.05.05** | **€** |
|---|---|
| Rent of conacre | 11,145 |
| Animal foodstuffs | 17,400 |
| Rates | 1,005 |
| Wages | 5,770 |
| Vet fees | 2,785 |
| Fertilisers | 1,335 |
| Light and heat | 888 |
| Hire of equipment and machinery | 4,450 |
| Seeds | 332 |
| Telephone | 449 |
| Contractor | 2,500 |

You are given the following additional information as at 31 May 2005:

*(i) Rent receivable due* *€225*
*(ii) Rates prepaid* *€205*
*(iii) Wages due* *€330*
*(iv) Light and heat due* *€162*

## 5.3 BALANCE SHEET

- Records the assets and liabilities of the farm
- Similar format to the Balance Sheet of a firm
- Adjustments (accruals and prepayments) are included
- A profit or loss is added to or subtracted from the capital

### Comprehensive Example

Frank and Mandy own a mixed farm in Rush. They have supplied you with the following information and ask you to prepare the following:

(a) *Income and Expenditure Account* for the year ending 31 December 1999
(b) *Balance Sheet* as at 31 December 1999

| Income for the year | IR£ | Expenditure for the year | IR£ |
|---|---|---|---|
| Cattle | 22,000 | Wages | 17,500 |
| Milk | 13,500 | Feed | 6,000 |
| Sheep | 8,250 | Electricity | 7,750 |
| Poultry | 5,550 | Insurance | 2,500 |
| | | Fertiliser | 1,350 |
| | | New tractor | 8,000 |
| | | Repairs | 1,150 |
| | | Rent | 1,550 |

| Assets | IR£ | Liabilities | IR£ |
|---|---|---|---|
| Land | 100,000 | Loan | 50,000 |
| Buildings | 44,000 | Creditors | 500 |
| Debtors | 1,300 | Drawings | 1,500 |
| Bank | 7,500 | Capital | 101,000 |
| Cash | 700 | | |

You are given the following additional information as at 31 Dec. 1999:

*(i) Wages due IR£500*
*(ii) Insurance prepaid IR£500*
*(iii) The new tractor is to be depreciated by 5%*

*SOLUTION*

| Income and Expenditure Account of Frank and Mandy for the year ended 31 December 1999 | | | |
|---|---|---|---|
| **Income** | **IR£** | **IR£** | **IR£** |
| Cattle | | 22,000 | |
| Milk | | 13,500 | |
| Sheep | | 8,250 | |
| Poultry | | 5,550 | |
| **Total Income** | | | 49,300 |
| **Less Expenditure** | | | |
| Wages | 17,500 | | |
| Add Wages Due | 500 | 18,000 | |
| Feed | | 6,000 | |
| Electricity | | 7,750 | |
| Insurance | 2,500 | | |
| Less Insurance Prepaid | 500 | 2,000 | |
| Fertiliser | | 1,350 | |
| Repairs | | 1,150 | |
| Rent | | 1,550 | |
| Depreciation Tractor | | 400 | |
| **Total Expenditure** | | | 38,200 |
| **Farm Profit** | | | 11,100 |

| Balance Sheet of Frank and Mandy as at 31 December 1999 | | | |
|---|---|---|---|
| | IR£ | IR£ | IR£ |
| **Fixed Assets** | **Cost** | **Deprec.** | **NBV** |
| Land | 100,000 | - | 100,000 |
| Buildings | 44,000 | - | 44,000 |
| Machinery | 8,000 | 400 | 7,600 |
| | 152,000 | 400 | 151,600 |
| **Current Assets** | | | |
| Debtors | | 1,300 | |
| Bank | | 7,500 | |
| Cash | | 700 | |
| Insurance Prepaid | | 500 | |
| | | 10,000 | |
| **Less Current Liabilities** | | | |
| Creditors | 500 | | |
| Wages due | 500 | 1,000 | |
| Working capital | | | 9,000 |
| **Total Net Assets** | | | 160,600 |
| **Financed By:** | | | |
| Capital | | 101,000 | |
| Add Farm Profit | | 11,100 | |
| | | 112,100 | |
| Less Drawings | | 1,500 | |
| | | | 110,600 |
| **Long-Term Liabilities** | | | |
| Loan | | | 50,000 |
| **Capital Employed** | | | 160,600 |

## 5.4 COMBINATION QUESTIONS

1. The Hill brothers own a farm in Co. Donegal. They have supplied you with the following information and ask you to prepare the following:

   (a) *Income and Expenditure Account* for the year ended 31 Dec. 2000
   (b) *Balance Sheet* as at 31 December 2000

| Income for the year | IR£ | Expenditure for the year | IR£ |
|---|---|---|---|
| Livestock | 27,450 | Wages | 19,900 |
| Grain | 23,560 | Feed | 13,330 |
| Sheep | 9,950 | Light and Heat | 4,190 |
| Fruit and Vegetables | 4,460 | Insurance | 3,530 |
| | | Fertiliser and Seeds | 2,440 |
| | | New farm machinery | 16,000 |
| | | Repairs | 3,450 |
| | | Rent and Rates | 2,700 |
| | | Loan Interest | 600 |

| Assets | IR£ | Liabilities | IR£ |
|---|---|---|---|
| Land | 120,000 | Loan | 40,000 |
| Buildings | 50,000 | Creditors | 3,500 |
| Machinery | 12,000 | Capital | 147,000 |
| Debtors | 4,350 | | |
| Bank | 1,530 | | |
| Cash | 1,900 | | |

You are given the following additional information as at 31 Dec. 2000:

*(i) Insurance due* *IR£470*
*(ii) Rent and rates prepaid* *IR£200*
*(iii) The new farm machinery is to be depreciated by 10%*

2. Louise O'Dwyer runs a farm in Co. Cork. She has supplied you with the following information and asks you to prepare the following:

(a) *Income and Expenditure Account* for the year ended 31 Dec. 2003
(b) *Balance Sheet* as at 31 December 2003

| Income for the year | € | Expenditure for the year | € |
|---|---|---|---|
| Barley | 14,470 | Wages | 4,345 |
| Wheat | 13,540 | Fertiliser | 2,470 |
| Oats | 3,900 | Seeds | 2,120 |
| Rent receivable | 4,400 | Insurance | 1,345 |
| | | Telephone | 885 |
| | | New farm equipment | 7,000 |
| | | Repairs | 2,340 |
| | | Rates | 1,300 |
| | | Loan Interest | 1,200 |

| Assets | € | Liabilities | € |
|---|---|---|---|
| Land | 100,000 | Bank Overdraft | 2,360 |
| Buildings | 30,000 | Creditors | 685 |
| Equipment | 5,000 | Capital | 90,000 |
| Debtors | 1,350 | Loan | 30,000 |

You are given the following additional information as at 31 Dec. 2003:

*(i) Rent receivable due* *€600*
*(ii) Rates due* *€200*
*(iii) Insurance prepaid* *€500*
*(iv) The new farm equipment is to be depreciated by 10%*

3. Pat and Patricia Walsh are farmers and have kept double-entry accounts. They have extracted the following Trial Balance on 31.12.05.

   You are required to prepare:

   (a) An *Income and Expenditure Account* for the year ended 31.12.05
   (b) A *Balance Sheet* as at 31.12.05

| Trial Balance as at 31 December 2005 | | | |
|---|---|---|---|
| | | DR € | CR € |
| Land and Buildings | | 150,000 | |
| Machinery | | 20,000 | |
| Debtors | | 3,500 | |
| Sales | Cattle | | 23,000 |
| | Sheep | | 18,580 |
| | Poultry | | 7,690 |
| Rent | | 8,500 | |
| Rates | | 3,500 | |
| Telephone | | 1,000 | |
| Insurance | | 1,100 | |
| Light and Heat | | 775 | |
| Fertiliser | | 2,230 | |
| Vet fees | | 885 | |
| Creditors | | | 2,220 |
| Loan | | | 40,000 |
| Capital | | | 100,000 |
| | | 191,490 | 191,490 |

The following matters must also be taken into consideration:

*(i) Rent due* *€500*
*(ii) Insurance prepaid* *€100*
*(iii) Depreciate* *Land and Buildings by 2%*
*Machinery by 10%*

4. Thomas Doyle, a farmer, has kept double-entry accounts. He has extracted the Trial Balance shown on 31.12.06.

   You are required to prepare:

   (a) An *Income and Expenditure Account* for the year ended 31.12.06
   (b) A *Balance Sheet* as at 31.12.06

The additional information is supplied at the year-end:

*(i) Rent receivable prepaid* *€300*
*(ii) Wages due* *€200*
*(iii) Insurance prepaid* *€350*
*(iv) Depreciate the machinery by 10%*

| Trial Balance as at 31 December 2006 | | |
|---|---|---|
| | DR € | CR € |
| Land and Buildings | 80,000 | |
| Machinery | 10,000 | |
| Debtors | 500 | |
| Sales Sheep | | 3,620 |
| Wool | | 1,690 |
| Cattle | | 2,580 |
| Rent receivable | | 1,300 |
| Rates | 1,500 | |
| Feed | 3,770 | |
| Insurance | 1,350 | |
| ESB | 250 | |
| Fertiliser | 230 | |
| Wages | 1,800 | |
| Creditors | | 210 |
| Loan | | 20,000 |
| Capital | | 70,000 |
| | 99,400 | 99,400 |

# CHAPTER 6
# BANK RECONCILIATION STATEMENTS

## Introduction

An individual who has a current account (cheque book account) keeps a record of all transactions in the **Household Bank Account** (Personal Bank Account). At regular intervals the bank sends the account holder a **Bank Statement.** This provides details of all transactions (lodgements and payments) that have been processed through the customer's bank account over a given period of time.

## Purpose of Bank Reconciliation

At a given date, the balance on the account holder's personal records and the balance as shown on the bank statement will seldom agree. Reasons for these different balances include:

(a) Cheques written by the account holder have been entered in his/her personal records but they have not yet been presented to the bank for payment, therefore they are not reflected in the bank account statement balance.

(b) Lodgements made by the individual may not have cleared into his/her bank account by the time the statement is prepared. This can arise for example, if cheques are lodged, the bank may wait until they have cleared the clearing system. This is to ensure that the drawer of the cheque has sufficient funds for it to be paid.

(c) The account holder will not have entered some transactions into his/her personal bank account such as direct debits, standing orders, credit transfers, current account fees, cheque book duties and other bank charges.

A **Bank Reconciliation Statement** is then prepared:

- ► In order to reconcile the two differing balances as per the household account and the bank statement
- ► To help check the accuracy of the bank statement and personal records and locate any errors
- ► To monitor all direct debits, standing orders, credit transfers and other bank/government charges

## Personal/Household Bank Accounts

In the personal/household bank account, individuals should have records of the following information each month:

(a) Opening Balance (how much money he/she has at the beginning of the month — the closing balance from last month's reconciliation statement)
(b) Any lodgements made (these increase the balance)
(c) Any withdrawals or payments made (these decrease the balance)
(d) Closing Balance (how much he/she has left at the end of the month — next month's opening balance)

This information can be presented in TWO different formats:

(i) T-Account
(ii) Continuous Balance

*T-Account Format*

| DR | Bank Account of Mr M. Dagg | | | | | | CR |
|---|---|---|---|---|---|---|---|
| Dec 1 | Balance | b/d | 300 | Dec 2 | Car Loan | SO | 200 |
| 1 | Salary | | 1,000 | 4 | Roches Stores | 002 | 300 |
| 26 | Lodgement | 13 | 300 | 6 | ATM — Main St. | | 100 |
| | | | | 21 | Car Repairs | 003 | 50 |
| | | | | 28 | Balance | c/d | 950 |
| | | | 1,600 | | | | 1,600 |
| 31 | Balance | b/d | 950 | | | | |

*Continuous Balance Format*

| Bank Account of Mr M. Dagg | | | | |
|---|---|---|---|---|
| **Date** | **Details** | **DR** | **CR** | **Balance** |
| Dec 1 | Balance | | | 300 |
| Dec 1 | Salary | 1,000 | | 1,300 |
| Dec 2 | Car Loan SO | | 200 | 1,100 |
| Dec 4 | Roches Stores 002 | | 300 | 800 |
| Dec 5 | ATM — Main St. | | 100 | 700 |
| Dec 21 | Car Repairs 003 | | 50 | 650 |
| Dec 26 | Lodgement | 300 | | 950 |

## The Bank Statement

Every two months (more often if requested) banks send their customers a Bank Statement. This is a record of all transactions that have been processed through his/her account in the bank. It is important to remember that this statement represents a summary of the customer's transactions in the bank's account. This helps explain why payments made are debited and payments lodged are credited in the bank's records. This is why a debit balance represents a **bank overdraft** because from the bank's point of view the customer is a debtor (current asset) he/she owes the bank money. Below is summary of all transactions as they would appear on the bank statement

*Figure 6.1*

1) BANK Statement
2) Procedure
- Balance
- Add Lodgements
- Less Cheques
- Equals Balance as per adjusted BANK Account

| Date | Details | [illegible] | [illegible] | Balance |
|---|---|---|---|---|
| | | | | How Much Money is in the Bank Account or owed to the Bank |
| | | | Decreases an overdraft | |

*Example*

| Mr. M Dagg<br>12 Cootehill Road<br>Cavan | | **Bank Statement**<br>Ulster Bank<br>Main Street<br>Cavan | Branch Code<br>Account Number<br>Statement Number<br>Date of Statement | 93–25–89<br>48535552<br>5<br>31.12.99 |
|---|---|---|---|---|
| **Date** | **Details** | **DR** | **CR** | **Balance** |
| Dec 1 | Balance | | | 300 |
| Dec 2 | Lodgement | | 1,000 | 1,300 |
| Dec 2 | Car Loan — SO | 200 | | 1,100 |
| Dec 2 | Bank Charges | 4 | | 1,096 |
| Dec 4 | Cheque — 002 | 300 | | 796 |
| Dec 6 | ATM — Dogsville | 100 | | 696 |
| Dec 12 | Government Duty — Cheque Book | 6 | | 690 |

From the above examples there is a difference between Mr M. Dagg's own bank account balance and his bank statement. Therefore a **Bank Reconciliation Statement** is prepared in order to reconcile the difference and produce the true bank balance.

## Procedure

Steps to Follow:

(i) On receipt of the bank statement compare it with the personal/household bank account. Any transactions, which are entered in both, are ticked (✔) — see Table 132 following

(ii) Mark any transactions, which only appear in one or other with an X (✘). These items contribute towards the difference between the two records and must be reconciled — see Table 132 following

(iii) Adjust the Bank Account with the items marked with an (✘) in the Bank Statement and balance it — see Table 133 following

(iv) Adjust the Bank Statement with the items marked with an (✘) in the Personal/Household Bank Account using the following layout (see Table 134 following):

**Balance** as per Bank Statement
**Add** lodgements not yet credited
**Less** cheques paid, not yet presented for payment
**Equals** Balance as per adjusted Bank Account

This account is called the **Bank Reconciliation Statement.**

The Balance on the two adjusted accounts should now agree and this is the true financial position of the individual.

**Question**
From the previous given example prepare:

(a) An *adjusted bank account*
(b) A *bank reconciliation statement.*

*SOLUTION*

*Steps (i) and (ii)*

| Bank Account of Mr M. Dagg | | | | | | | | | |
|---|---|---|---|---|---|---|---|---|---|
| Dec 1 | Balance | b/d | ✔ | 300 | Dec 2 | Car Loan | SO | ✔ | 200 |
| 1 | Salary | | ✔ | 1,000 | 4 | Roches Stores | 002 | ✔ | 300 |
| 26 | Lodgement | 13 | × | 300 | 6 | ATM — Main St. | | ✔ | 100 |
| | | | | | 21 | Car Repairs | 003 | × | 50 |
| | | | | | 28 | Balance | c/d | | 950 |
| | | | | 1,600 | | | | | 1,600 |
| Mar 1 | Balance | b/d | | 950 | | | | | |

| Mr. M Dagg<br>12 Cootehill Road<br>Cavan | **Bank Statement**<br>Ulster Bank<br>Main Street<br>Cavan | Branch Code<br>Account Number<br>Statement Number<br>Date of Statement | 93–25–89<br>48535552<br>5<br>31.12.99 |
|---|---|---|---|

| **Date** | **Details** | | **DR** | | **CR** | **Balance** |
|---|---|---|---|---|---|---|
| Dec 1 | Balance | | | ✔ | | 300 |
| Dec 2 | Lodgement | | | ✔ | 1,000 | 1,300 |
| Dec 2 | Car Loan — SO | ✔ | 200 | | | 1,100 |
| Dec 2 | Bank Charges | ✘ | 4 | | | 1,096 |
| Dec 4 | Cheque — 002 | ✔ | 300 | | | 796 |
| Dec 6 | ATM — Main Street | ✔ | 100 | | | 696 |
| Dec 12 | Government Duty - Cheque Book | ✘ | 6 | | | 690 |

*Step (iii)*

| **DR** | | **ADJUSTED BANK ACCOUNT** | | | | | **CR** |
|---|---|---|---|---|---|---|---|
| Dec 31 | Balance | b/d | 950 | Dec 2 | Bank Charges | | 4 |
| | | | | Dec 12 | Cheque Duty | | 6 |
| | | | | Dec 31 | Adj. Balance | c/d | 940 |
| | | | 950 | | | | 950 |
| Jan 1 | Adj. Balance | b/d | 940 | | | | |

*Step (iv)*

| **BANK RECONCILIATION STATEMENT AS AT 31 DECEMBER 1999** | |
|---|---|
| **Balance** as per **Bank Statement** | 690 |
| **Add** Lodgements not yet credited | 300 |
| | 990 |
| **Less** Cheques written not yet presented for payment (cashed) — Car repairs | 50 |
| **Balance** as per **Adjusted Bank Account** | 940 |

The adjusted balance tells us that Mr M. Dagg really has IR£940 left in his account.

## Practice Questions

1. Bríd O'Mara has a current account with the Ulster Bank. She received this bank statement on 31 March 1997.

| Bríd O'Mara<br>Oak Lawn<br>Celbridge | **Bank Statement**<br>Ulster Bank<br>Celbridge<br>Co. Kildare | Branch Code<br>Account Number<br>Statement Number<br>Date of Statement | 91–63–24<br>473815<br>73<br>31.3.97 | |
|---|---|---|---|---|
| **Date 1997** | **Details** | **DR** | **CR** | **Balance** |
| Mar 1 | Balance forward | | | 157DR |
| Mar 9 | Cheque 454 | 84 | | 241DR |
| Mar 10 | Lodgement | | 879 | 638 |
| Mar 11 | A.T.M. | 59 | | 579 |
| Mar 13 | Cheque 452 | 124 | | 455 |
| Mar 16 | SO E.B.S | 118 | | 337 |
| Mar 18 | Credit Transfer | | 93 | 430 |
| Mar 22 | DD Telecom | 57 | | 373 |
| Mar 25 | Cheque 455 | 88 | | 285 |
| Mar 30 | Current A/C fees | 8 | | 277 |
| Mar 31 | Interest | 6 | | 271 |

The following is Bríd's own account of her bank transactions. Compare this Bank Account/Cash Book with the bank statement above and:

(i) Prepare an *Adjusted Bank Account/Cash Account* for Bríd
(ii) Prepare a *Bank Reconciliation Statement* as at 31 March 1997

**Bank Account/Cash Book of Bríd O'Mara**

| | | | | | | | |
|---|---|---|---|---|---|---|---|
| Mar 7 | Salary | | 879 | Mar 1 | Balance | Chq | 157 |
| Mar 31 | Sale of bike | | 45 | Mar 5 | T Nolan | 452 | 124 |
| | | | | Mar 6 | Foley's | 453 | 87 |
| | | | | Mar 8 | Car Repairs | 454 | 84 |
| | | | | Mar 11 | A.T.M | | 59 |
| | | | | Mar 16 | SO E.B.S. | | 118 |
| | | | | Mar 21 | Insurance | 455 | 88 |
| | | | | Mar 31 | Balance | c/d | 207 |
| | | | 924 | | | | 924 |
| Mar 31 | Balance | b/d | 207 | | | | |

2. Duffy Ltd opened a current account in the Ulster Bank on 1 May 1996 and lodged IR£700. The following transactions took place during May.

| *May* | | *No.* | *IR£* |
|---|---|---|---|
| *2* | *Paid suppliers by cheque* | *1* | *550* |
| *6* | *Purchased stock by cheque* | *2* | *360* |
| *9* | *Paid ESB by cheque* | *3* | *140* |
| *11* | *Paid insurance by cheque* | *4* | *120* |
| *16* | *Cash sales lodged* | | *1,600* |
| *19* | *Paid Jones Ltd by cheque* | *5* | *1,900* |
| *28* | *Lodged to account* | | *1,700* |
| *30* | *Paid Telecom by cheque* | *6* | *320* |
| *31* | *Cash sales lodged* | | *1,450* |

They received this bank statement on 31 May 1996.

| **Bank Statement for Duffy Ltd** | | | | |
|---|---|---|---|---|
| **Date 1996** | **Details** | **DR** | **CR** | **Balance** |
| May 1 | Lodgement | | 700 | 700 |
| May 5 | Cheque 1 | 550 | | 150 |
| May 10 | Cheque 3 | 140 | | 10 |
| May 14 | Cheque 4 | 120 | | 110 DR |
| May 16 | Lodgement | | 1,600 | 1,490 |
| May 18 | Cheque 2 | 360 | | 1,130 |
| May 24 | Standing Order | 400 | | 730 |
| May 26 | Credit Transfer | | 550 | 1,280 |
| May 28 | Lodgement | | 1,700 | 2,980 |
| May 30 | Current Account Fees | 25 | | 2,955 |

From the above information:

(i) Prepare Duffy Ltd's *Bank Account* for the month of May

(ii) Compare Duffy's Bank Account with the Bank Statement then prepare an *Adjusted Bank Account*

(iii) Prepare a *Bank Reconciliation Statement* as on 31 May 1996

(Adapted from Junior Certificate 1996 Higher Level, PII, Q6)

3. Michael Lynch has a current account with the Bank of Ireland. He received this bank statement on 30 March 1992.

| Michael Lynch<br>13 Woodlands Park<br>Palmerstown<br>Dublin 20 | **Bank Statement**<br>BANK OF IRELAND | Branch Code<br>Account Number<br>Statement Number<br>Date of Statement | | 90-07-62<br>74107628<br>70<br>30.3.92 |
|---|---|---|---|---|
| **Date 1992** | **Details** | **DR** | **CR** | **Balance** |
| Feb 28 | Balance forward | | | 1,081 |
| Mar 8 | Cheque 393 | 126 | | 955 |
| Mar 10 | Cheque 392 | 54 | | 901 |
| Mar 11 | Credit Transfer | | 100 | 1,001 |
| Mar 13 | A.T.M | 150 | | 851 |
| Mar 20 | First N.B.S. SO | 160 | | 691 |
| Mar 22 | Irish Life DD | 68 | | 623 |
| Mar 27 | Cheque 395 | 120 | | 503 |
| Mar 29 | Current Account Fees | 6 | | 497 |

The following is Michael Lynch's own account of his bank transactions. Compare this account with the bank statement above and:

(i) Prepare an *Adjusted Bank Account/Cash Account* for M. Lynch
(ii) Prepare a *Bank Reconciliation Statement* as at 31 March 1992

**Bank Account/Cash Book of Michael Lynch**

| | | | | | | | |
|---|---|---|---|---|---|---|---|
| Feb 28 | Balance | | 1,081 | Mar 1 | ESB | 392 | 54 |
| Mar 30 | Lodgement | | 355 | Mar 6 | ELF Garage | 393 | 126 |
| | | | | Mar 13 | Cash ATM | | 150 |
| | | | | Mar 20 | First N.B.S. | SO | 160 |
| | | | | Mar 22 | Irish Life | DD | 68 |
| | | | | Mar 27 | Shopwell Ltd | 394 | 75 |
| | | | | Mar 28 | Mulligan's Shop | 395 | 120 |
| | | | | Mar 30 | Balance | c/d | 683 |
| | | | 1,436 | | | | 1,436 |
| Mar 31 | Balance | b/d | 683 | | | | |

(Adapted from Junior Certificate 1992 Higher Level, PI, Section B, Q4)